QUILT LOCAL

Finding Inspiration
in the Everyday
(with 40 projects)

HEATHER JONES

photography by
JENNY HALLENGREN

foreword by
DENYSE SCHMIDT

stc craft / a melanie falick book / new york

contents

FOREWORD DENYSE SCHMIDT

In 2011, the Modern Quilt Guild asked me to jury its "Project Modern" challenge. I was to choose my favorite quilt from photographs the finalists had provided, along with written essays about their inspiration and process. A daunting task to be sure, but among the many stunning entries, one visually arresting quilt stood out for its subtle color palette and simple, straightforward design that had clarity and strength. "Who made this?" I wondered, and "Where did this design come from?" That was my introduction to the amazing work of Heather Jones.

Heather's story of that particular quilt, and her way of working in general, confirmed what I suspected: Here was a true artist with a unique vision and the talent and discipline to hone her expression of that vision. I loved that she found her inspiration in the humble, everyday things around her, like in the vernacular architecture of the old farm buildings dotting the landscape where she lives. Like so many quilters over the last centuries who have created patterns based on household implements and rituals that have defined their environment, Heather sees a rhythmic pattern in the sheathing of a farm silo she passes every day and graphic beauty in the painted lines in the parking lot at a big box store. Heather notices details that most of us may overlook—layers of structural details in an old general store brick wall, the juxtaposition of color in a modern skyscraper, or the irregular pattern of tile in a restroom—and transforms these into striking works of textile art. She brings a fresh perspective to quilting. Subtly informed by her art training and experience, Heather's work is rooted in an authentic expression that is uniquely her own, while embracing the historical and cultural resonance of the medium.

I know how deceptively difficult it is to produce work that is restrained. When I began making quilts, the medium had an ingrained habit of "more is more." It can be easy to impress with virtuoso sewing skills, use of abundant and vibrant color, and complicated visual tricks. Plenty of prints and patchwork can distract our attention, but it is much more skillful—and brave—to find the purest expression of form, to let the poetry of composition and color have its say, to not overcomplicate or muddle the message with needless flourishes. The results, as seen in Heather's quilts, are breathtaking in their stark beauty, and they can engage our interest for a lifetime.

With *Quilt Local*, Heather shares beautiful quilt designs that you will enjoy making again and again. She also generously provides a practical, easy roadmap to developing your own creative voice: simple daily habits you can practice to remain open and present to the inspiration that surrounds you, and accessible ways of understanding and working with color. Heather shares her methods of working in a way that will have you seeing your world with new eyes and finding the inspiration to bring your authentic voice to your own creations.

OPPOSITE Detail of colorway 1 of the Eden Park quilt on page 106, a design inspired by wall tiles in the Cincinnati Art Museum.

INTRODUCTION

I didn't grow up in a family of quilters. My maternal great-great-aunt Ollie quilted, but she was the only one. I was, however, lucky enough to know her, because she lived with my grandparents for a few years when I was a child, and I owe my love of quilts to her. Throughout my youth I spent hours making things by hand, from weaving potholders on those little looms that were so popular in the '70s and '80s to making mud pots in my backyard to sculpting proper clay ones in ceramics classes after school. My passion for studio art really bloomed in junior high and high school, though, and I was fortunate to have two very wonderful art teachers who helped me hone my fine-art skills. As a teen I often spent any money I had at the art supply store on watercolors and pastels, my two favorite media at the time.

After a brief stint in a pre-med program, I majored in art history in college and graduate school. While most of my classes focused on the history of art and art theory, I continued to take as many studio art classes as possible. It was around this time that I also began to work regularly with fiber and fabrics and to sew.

As is often the case with artists and designers, I bring all of my past experiences with me when I approach quilting. I work more from a fine art perspective than a traditional quilting one. While I greatly respect the art of traditional quilt making, and some of my favorite quilts are vintage ones that I've picked up over the years, I'm more interested in creating quilts that don't look like ones I have seen before. I'm often inspired by everyday places and things that many people wouldn't even notice, and I'm always excited by the challenge to translate that inspiration into my work.

When I decided to write a book about quilting, I knew that I wanted it to be different than anything else that had been published. One of the first quilting projects that I ever designed and made was inspired by a painted grid in the parking lot of a local superstore, which is my Mason quilt on page 44. That project really had a profound impact on my life as a designer and quilt maker, and it made me look at my local surroundings in a different way. I had such a great time throughout the entire creative process of making that quilt, from finding such a striking graphic design in an unexpected place, to incorporating that inspiration into my sketches and, ultimately, my finished quilt. While I continue to create work in a number of styles today, the process of finding unique inspiration in my everyday life is the most rewarding to me.

Because the projects in these pages have all been inspired by my environment and local surroundings, this book has become somewhat of a celebration of Ohio, my home state, and more specifically the towns and communities around me. But I truly believe that there is beauty everywhere, no matter the surroundings, and I hope that you use the tools in this book to help you find beauty and inspiration in your locale as well.

My quilts are often made entirely from solid-colored cottons, and people frequently remark on the colors that I choose and the ways in which I create color palettes. With my background in art history and fine art, I felt it was important to share my knowledge of color theory and color interaction and how I use them in my designs, so a large portion of the book is devoted to this as well.

In Chapter 1, I introduce how I find inspiration in everyday places, and I also share five habits that I find to be very useful when looking for design ideas. In Chapter 2, I address the basics of color theory, which are very helpful to know when creating color palettes and color stories in quilting—and any other type of creative work. In Chapter 3, I share my process of translating inspiration into finished quilts, using sketches and simple math. Chapter 4 includes a thorough overview of basic quilt construction techniques, from fabric preparation and cutting to finishing and binding.

And then come my quilts. I designed eighteen quilts for this book, plus two pillow covers and a series of nine quilt blocks to demonstrate specific concepts and design applications of color theory. Many of the patterns are quite easy to construct, but all have a very strong visual component, which has become the hallmark of my minimalist quilting style.

For many years I was intimidated by the process of quilt making, so I hope this book helps others to understand that beautiful quilts don't have to be difficult to construct.

You will notice that I am presenting two distinct colorways for each quilt. I decided to do this in order to illustrate how different the same layout can look when you change the fabric colors. In some cases, the color palette that I chose for the first version of the design was inspired by the actual colors of the object or place that inspired it. For others, I created the palette from scratch. In the introduction to each set of instructions, I explain my choices. In turn, each project and unique color palette is also a mini lesson in color theory and fabric selection.

As a designer, it always interests me to see how quilters interpret my patterns. So, of course, I'd love to see how you make the quilts in this book in your own colorways, or equally—if not more—exciting: how you design quilts based on inspiration that is local to you. You can always reach me through my blog, oliveandollie.com, or my website, heatherjonesstudio.com

While my work is considered by many people to be modern in aesthetic, I feel that in some ways, it is actually quite traditional. For hundreds of years quilt makers have been inspired by places and objects in their everyday lives. Think of Churn Dash, Rail Fence, Flying Geese, Log Cabin, and hundreds of other quilt patterns developed in the past. The (mostly) women who made these quilts had a desire to create beautiful, functional objects, and drew upon what they saw in their daily lives as sources of inspiration for their work. I am honored to carry on that tradition.

PART 1 PROCESS

chapter 1

FINDING INSPIRATION

I believe that inspiration is everywhere. It sounds like a cliché, but it's true. Inspiration can come from the insect that lands near a porch light, from the sunset at dusk, from an abandoned brick building downtown, and, literally, from everything in between. This type of inspiration excites me because it catches the imagination unexpectedly and can lead each of us down our own creative path. What appears to one person to be nothing more than an uninhabited brick building can be the starting point of a beautiful graphic design to another. I might be drawn to the lines created by the pattern of the bricks in a building's construction. You might look at the same building and become captivated by the color of the bricks themselves, a dark orange red, contrasted with the pale blue sky.

HOW I LOOK FOR INSPIRATION

We all lead such busy lives these days, so it's nice to know that we don't need to go anywhere special for inspiration. I am married and have two young children, which means I spend a lot of time working around the house, driving the kids to and from school and other activities, and running errands. Perhaps it isn't surprising then that one of the first quilts I designed for this book, the Mason quilt on page 44, was inspired by the grid in the parking lot at a local big box store. Although I certainly wasn't looking for inspiration from that location that day, I was suddenly struck by the graphic quality of the painted lines that make up the yield sign in the parking lot in front of the entrance.

Similarly, my Indian Hill quilt on page 146 is based on the layout of the decking on a friend's dock. I've been on that dock and in the pond it serves many times since I was a child, but one day recently I noticed the intricate pattern created by the slats of wood.

Knowing that I can find inspiration everywhere doesn't mean I don't want to visit art museums or travel far and wide for inspiration. Of course, I want to do that as well. But I realize that I don't have to wait to see an exhibition of Picassos or climb the Alps to feel inspired. In fact, looking for inspiration while driving to the grocery store—or even pushing the grocery cart around—can make some mundane tasks more interesting.

Over the years I've developed four every-day habits that help me find inspiration and keep track of it. I'm happy to share what I've learned, and I hope that it will benefit you.

OPPOSITE Some of the inspirations for my designs: architectural details, street markings, and an antique quilt.

HABIT 1
be aware

First, it's incredibly important to be aware of your surroundings when you're looking for design inspiration. Being aware is a muscle that needs to work to get stronger, and it does take some discipline.

Literally, keep your eyes open and pay attention to everything around you, and particularly the things that stop you in your tracks. Take note of them. What is it about them that caused you to stop and look at them? Is it the color, the texture, the design, or the layout? Maybe it's a graphic quality that you see painted on a grid in a parking lot, or the juxtaposition of two colors together on a moth's wing. Maybe it's the color of fresh blueberries being folded into batter while you are baking, and the way they bring a blue marbled swirl to what was purely a creamy white substance. Whatever it is, make a mental note of it.

HABIT 2
stay present

If I feel myself getting distracted a lot, I know I must find some time to be quiet and alone. This is usually only an option early in the morning or late at night when the rest of the family is asleep. I prefer getting up early in the morning, and while it's not always fun to wake up at 5am, I relish those few hours before the sun comes up and the rest of the family starts stirring.

Although meditation certainly helps a lot of people unwind and clear their minds, I don't regularly meditate myself. But I do try to quiet my mind through creating. Sketching is very meditative to me, and it also allows me to explore ideas and designs that I'm working on in my studio. My mind doesn't shut off easily, but I find that I can reboot it, so to speak, by spending a

bit of time with my sketchbook every day. Many people say that yoga or exercise classes, or quiet walks in nature, help them stay present. Figure out what works for you and then be sure to fit it into your life.

HABIT 3
be open to surprising sources of inspiration

Take the time to look at your environment, no matter what it is or where it is. Put your smart phone down and check out the scenery, whether it's urban, rural, or somewhere in between. Whether you're inside or outside, on a special vacation in an exotic place or doing a mundane chore in your neighborhood, there are beautiful colors and patterns literally everywhere, even in places where you least expect them. Have you ever looked at the installation of paint chips at the hardware store? That is one of my favorite places to play with color and color combinations. There are usually hundreds of paint swatches that you can take, at no charge. You can easily build a color swatch library by taking a few every time you visit the hardware store and then refer to them at home when you're ready to create a project.

Look with an open mind. Don't force yourself to try to find inspiration. In my experience, the harder you try to look for something to inspire you, the more difficult it is to be inspired. Instead, relax and put your mind at ease. Take a few minutes to walk around, or drive around, and just look at the things you see. You may surprise yourself to find that you spy something new, even in a place that you may have been to hundreds of times before.

HABIT 4
take photos and notes

I just told you to put down your smart phones so you could be more fully in the moment and open to the possibilities of being inspired by your surroundings, but now I'm going to ask you to pick them up again. Smart phones are incredibly useful for the purposes of documenting and recording your inspiration. I always have my phone with me, and it has a great digital camera built into it, so I'm always ready to snap a quick photo with it. If the image is in a location that I want to make sure to remember, I'll make a quick note of it in my phone's note-taking app, too.

I also recommend carrying a sketchbook and a writing tool with you at all times. It doesn't have to be fancy, and it doesn't have to be big. Really, anything will do— you just need a designated place to jot down notes about something that catches your eye or to make a sketch of it. I typically begin my sketchbook drawings in pencil, and

I prefer mechanical pencils so that I always have a sharp point.

I use my sketchbooks as a way to document and keep track of shapes for designs, like the strong linear elements and repetition of rectangles that inspired my Columbus quilt on page 142. The margins around the drawings are filled with my notes, where I'll hash out ideas for colors and fabrics. I also explore the scale of a project that I'm working on in my sketchbook by making quick drawings of the overall design of the quilt. If I want to remember specific details about the inspiration behind a design, I will include that, too. Then, when I want to develop an idea from my sketchbook and bring it from inspiration to a finished quilt project, I use these sketches, doodles, and notes as starting points to my creative process.

chapter 2

AN IDIOSYNCRATIC LESSON
IN COLOR THEORY

Color theory, by definition, is the practical foundation to color mixing and the visual effects of specific color combinations. While the formal study of color theory can be quite scientific, I believe that we all have an intuitive sense of how color works. In this chapter I explain how I design my color palettes, and I offer tools that I hope will help you develop color schemes of your own.

I have provided two colorways for each quilt in this book to show you how changing colors affects them. You may choose to recreate the quilts using the exact colors that I have, but this chapter should give you the confidence to create your own unique color stories as well.

**FORMAL COLOR THEORY
AND THE INTERACTION OF COLOR**

My first experience with formal color theory was in my seventh-grade art class. I was taught about color order, using the acronym ROY G. BIV, which, of course, stands for Red, Orange, Yellow, Green, Blue, Indigo, and Violet. It's the sequence of hues that theoretically make up a rainbow, and many people are familiar with it. However, my greater knowledge of color theory comes from the work of Josef Albers, who is considered by many to be the modern expert on the subject. Born in Germany, Albers studied and later taught at the Bauhaus before eventually coming to America in 1933.

Albers may be known best for his works entitled *Homage to the Square*, a series of painted studies of quite simple subject matter—squares floating within larger squares—that explore the relationship between adjacent colors. This became the basis of his work for many years as he analyzed how, for example, a particular shade of orange works with a particular shade of brown and green. I've been lucky enough to see some of these paintings in person at art museums over the years, and I'm always struck by their simple beauty. In fact, I've designed quilts completely inspired by them, including my Homage pillow cover on page 152.

Albers published his findings about color theory in his book *The Interaction of Color* in 1963. This book has been an invaluable resource for countless people, in particular artists, designers, and educators, including myself, and I highly recommend it.

The Interaction of Color covers many theories on color, including color relativity, intensity, and temperature; vibrating and vanishing boundaries; and the illusion of transparency and reversed grounds. While these can be complex theories to grasp, I bet there are ones that you are familiar with, even if you have never studied color theory

OPPOSITE I designed Homage Blocks Nos. 1–9 to illustrate different types of color palettes. To use them to create pillow covers, see page 152.

HOMAGE BLOCKS IN 9 COLOR PALETTES

No. 1. ANALOGOUS

No. 2. COMPLEMENTARY

No. 3. MONOCHROMATIC

No. 4. NEUTRAL

No. 5. SECONDARY

No. 6. MUTED

No. 7. SATURATED

No. 8. COOL

No. 9. WARM

or don't know them by name. For instance, you have most likely experienced color relativity, particularly if you have blue eyes that sometimes look more green, especially if you are wearing a green shirt. This is an example of how colors are relative, that is to say, they are affected by other colors near them.

Most people are also acquainted with the notion that colors have a temperature associated with them—warm and cool. Another important aspect of color that you probably know about, regardless of your experience with formal color theory, is that color is perceived differently by everybody. What I see as a particular color, you may see totally differently. Color is subjective, and that is one of its beautiful qualities.

In 2013, in celebration of its 50th anniversary, *The Interaction of Color* was made available in a few different formats, including a paperback version, a hardcover complete edition that includes 145 full-color reproductions of Albers's original color plates, as well as an app for the iPad that allows the user to digitally experiment with his or her own color palettes. With the app, you can build upon the color experiments that Albers explores in his book and can recreate his examples at home digitally, using the same colors that he did in each one or an entirely new palette of custom hues. I frequently use the app as a quick way to build potential color palettes for quilting projects, or just for creative play. I think it's quite satisfying to play with color in a way that doesn't require a lot of art supplies or crafting materials, and this app is a perfect way to do that. The palettes that you create can be stored and later imported to a variety of design software for further exploration and use.

OPPOSITE Solid-colored fabric squares forming a classic color wheel, which echoes the colors of the rainbow.

THE COLOR WHEEL AND A COLOR VOCABULARY

The color wheel is an arrangement of colors in a circular design, based on how they appear in nature, that is, in rainbow order. It's a very useful tool for learning about colors and how they react with each other. Most color wheels have twelve segments of colors and a component that spins around that is useful for creating your own color palettes because it's a fast way to see color combinations and how they work together. Color wheels typically also include the following definitions:

PRIMARY COLORS: Red, yellow, and blue. These colors cannot be made from mixing other colors.

SECONDARY COLORS: Orange, green, and violet. These colors are made by mixing two primary colors together. (I've created a color palette using secondary colors in my Homage Block No. 5 on page 15—purple, orange, and green. The center of the block is a light lavender, the second tier of the block is an orange, and the final tier is a green.)

TERTIARY COLORS: Red-orange, yellow-orange, yellow-green, blue-green, blue-violet, and red-violet. Each of these colors is made by mixing a primary color with one of its adjacent secondary colors.

Some additional color terminology is useful to know and understand as well. For example, colors have temperature. WARM COLORS are associated with fire, including reds, oranges, and yellows. Homage Block No. 9 in red and two oranges exemplifies these warm colors.

COOL COLORS are associated with water, such as greens, blues, and violets. See my Homage Block No. 8 in blue, medium blue, and light blue.

NEUTRAL COLORS include white, black, and gray. My Homage Block No. 4 is an example of a neutral color palette with a cool white in the center, surrounded by tiers of a

warmer cream and gray. And something you should know about neutrals: theoretically, neutrals like white, gray, and black are just that, neutral. However, in reality, neutral-colored materials, including fabrics, paints, and other pigments, can have a temperature associated with them. Grays, in particular, are usually either warm or cool in color.

Colors are often described by three characteristics: HUE, VALUE, and INTENSITY. A hue is the name of a particular color on the color wheel, such as red. Value is a color's relative lightness or darkness, in reference to a ten-point gray scale; the lower the

value, the darker the color, and the higher the value, the lighter the color. Intensity, also known as saturation, is the purity of a color that determines its relative brightness or dullness; an intense or saturated color is one that is quite bright, while a muted color is one that is less intense or less saturated. A TINT is a color with the addition of white, so pink is a tint of red. A SHADE is a color with the addition of black, so maroon is a shade of red.

Homage Block No. 7 (violet, dark blue, print) is an example of a HIGH SATURATION color palette, consisting of a print with

No. 7. SATURATED

No. 6. MUTED

many saturated and intense colors in it, paired with saturated dark blue and violet solid fabrics. Homage Block No. 6 (white, pale blue, print) is an example of a muted color palette, because the colors in the fabrics are much less intense and saturated than the colors in the high saturation block. The neutral white combined with the pale blue and less intense print round out this muted color scheme.

A **COLOR PALETTE** or **COLOR SCHEME** is a set of colors that are used together. A **MONOCHROMATIC** color scheme is one in which one color, its tint, and its shade are used together. My Homage Block No. 3 on page 15 is an example of a monochromatic color scheme. I've placed a pale pink fabric in the center of the square, surrounded it with a mid-tone pink in the second tier, and have finished it with a saturated dark pink for the outer tier of the block.

COMPLEMENTARY COLORS are those that are directly across from each other on the color wheel. Red and green, yellow and violet, and orange and blue are complementary colors. Used together at full strength they can be challenging to look at because, as complementary colors, they pop against each other and clash. However, they can be used effectively in a design when one complementary color is used in a much smaller quantity than the other. Two complementary colors can also be used together with great success when the intensity of one of the colors is a muted tone.

Homage Block No. 2 (purple, violet, yellow) is an example of a complementary color scheme. I've placed a mid-tone yellow in the center of the square and surrounded it with a muted lavender in the second tier, finishing off the block with a more saturated purple to complete the color palette.

ANALOGOUS COLORS are those that are next to each other in a group on the color wheel. For example, blue, blue-green, and green are analogous colors. They are easier to work with together than complementary

NO. 2. COMPLEMENTARY

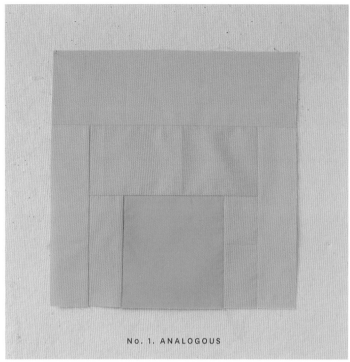

No. 1. ANALOGOUS

colors because they don't bounce off of each other as much and they are considered more harmonious.

My Homage Block No. 1 on page 15 is an example of an analogous color scheme because I've used green, a bluish green, and blue in the palette. The center square is a saturated Kelly green, paired with a muted celery green in the second tier, and finally a saturated robin's egg blue outer tier.

Color wheels are easy to find at art and craft supply stores and are a great addition to your crafting area at home. They are also handy to use when you are buying fabric and want to compare colors or quickly find the complement of something. When I designed the second version of my Third Street quilt (page 112), I wanted to create one in a complementary color scheme. The color wheel allowed me to easily find two colors, in this case turquoise blue and orange, to use as my color palette.

INTUITIVE COLOR THEORY

Basic knowledge about color theory is very important to have, but I think it's just as important to listen to your own intuition and develop your own voice as a colorist. We all have particular color stories that we are drawn to. My favorites tend to be muted and in the cool family, and I love to use lots of neutral colors in my designs as well.

I create my colors palettes with a variety of tools I keep in my studio: a color wheel, color swatch paint chips from the hardware store, marker pens, fabric swatch cards, and snips of fabric or other ephemera that catch my eye. I tend to draw a lot of color inspiration from nature and my everyday environment, and I often design quilts using fabrics that are similar in colors to the actual colors in the places and things that inspired them.

For example, for the Shellshock quilt on page 84, I was inspired by a painting of the same name by my husband, Jeff.

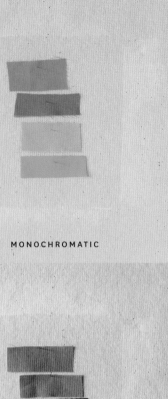

MONOCHROMATIC

COMPLEMENTARY

DIFFERENT VALUES

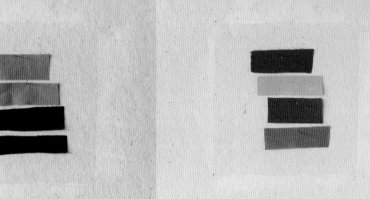

COMPLEMENTARY

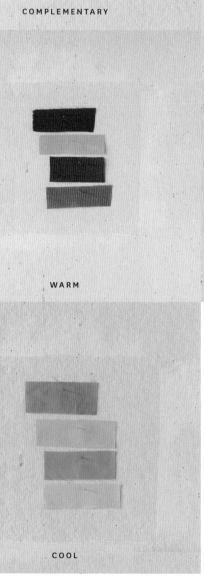

WARM

NEUTRAL/MONOCHROMATIC

COMPLEMENTARY

COOL

THIS PAGE Cutting snips of fabric and seeing how they react and relate to each other is a good way to find your favorite color stories. OPPOSITE Cotton fabrics are available in hundreds of different colors. Enjoy experimenting!

For my first version of Shellshock, I chose fabrics that nearly matched Jeff's painting—a warm cream fabric for the background and a brighter white and two shades of yellow for the center pieced section to convey the sense of color gradation in the painting.

My Red Lion quilt on page 90 was inspired by a nineteenth-century brick church that has great large windows with shutters. To suggest the painted shutters and brickwork in the inspiration, I used four shades of solid white cottons, ranging from pure bright white to warmer hues of cream, paired with a dark brown woven fabric.

For my first colorway of my Dayton quilt on page 76, I used the colors of the church inspiration as a starting point to create my palette, but I did not try to duplicate them. Using my own color sense, I chose an orange with red undertones for the background, which is much more intense than the true color of the bricks. For the cross in this quilt design, I chose a warm cream color with yellow undertones that I thought worked really well with the warm tone of the orange fabric.

Now that you are familiar with the basics of color theory, you should feel more confident about creating your own color palettes for your sewing projects. Have fun picking colors that you like, and feel free to choose whatever colors and palettes you are drawn to. I strongly believe that there is no right or wrong way to use color, no matter what colors you use. What is important is to use colors that you love and to feel free to experiment with colors in your own designs.

chapter 3

PROCESS—INSPIRATION TO QUILT DESIGN

I get really excited finding inspiration in everyday places and things, and I love the process, and challenge, of bringing that inspiration to life in my quilts. Here I explain how I work. I hope that once you understand how simple the process can be, you will feel excited about creating your own unique quilt designs. Use my tips and the basic tools that you probably already own as a starting point to develop your own creative process and to see what feels right to you. I can't wait to see what you create!

SKETCHING A QUILT DESIGN

As I explained in Chapter 1, I usually capture and document inspiration with my camera phone. When I set out to develop something that has inspired me into a finished quilt design, I retrieve the photograph and upload it to my computer. This allows me to see the photo on a larger scale, as well as zoom in and out on details. I typically do not edit the photograph at all, other than perhaps a bit of cropping, because I prefer to keep the colors and light of the image as they were when I shot it.

From the photograph, I develop a rough pencil drawing in a sketchbook. I like Rhodia Reverse Book sketchbooks. They come in a variety of sizes and styles, but my favorite one is the 8½" (22 cm) square format with a spiral binding. This type of binding allows the sketchbook to be opened easily and lay flat, which is really handy when I'm drawing. These sketchbooks also have a firm front and back cover, which give the paper support while I'm sketching. The paper is bright white and the square grid on it is printed in grayish blue ink—while the fine-line grid

is clearly visible, the ink is subtle and doesn't detract from or compete with what I draw over it. I also work with Rhodia's 8¼" x 11¾" (21 cm x 30 cm) notebooks if I'm creating a longer design. This style of sketchbook does not have a spiral binding, although it does have similar firm covers that can be flipped to the back for support. The paper in both of these types of sketchbooks is perforated, so the pages can be removed easily if necessary.

I prefer to sketch with mechanical pencils rather than wood pencils, and my favorites are Papermate Sharpwriter #2 pencils. The lead is smooth and produces a beautiful mark, ranging from light to dark depending on the pressure exerted. Also, the tips are always sharp, and the marks erase easily, which comes in handy, especially during the initial phases of sketching. I also use a separate eraser because I've found that the lead in these pencils often lasts longer than the eraser that is on the end of them. I use both Sanford Design 2000 Plastic Erasers and Paper Mate Black Pearl erasers, because they do not smear the graphite from my pencil drawings and do not leave a lot of debris on the paper either.

When I begin to sketch, I typically lay out a quick, rough drawing that is based on the inspiration. Here I'll determine what areas of the inspiration I want to emphasize in my final design. More often than not, I simplify what I see in the inspiration, which goes hand in hand with my minimal style of quilt making. Once I have a rough drawing I'm happy with down on paper, I begin to clean it up and refine it. I have a 6" (15 cm) ruler that I use when I want my drawn lines to be more precise. When my final design is roughed in, I go over every line with the pencil and ruler so that the lines are consistent and straight.

PLANNING QUILT SPECIFICS
size

To determine the size of the quilt, I use the squares of the graph paper and simple math to calculate. I typically use the ratio of each graph paper square being equal to 1", 2", 3", or 4" (2.5, 5, 7.5, or 10 cm), and I calculate the size of the quilt by adding up all of the squares on each side of the project. For example, my finished Caesar Creek quilt on page 96 measures 52" x 80" (130 cm x 200 cm), excluding the binding, and the sketch of the design on the graph paper measures 26 x 40 squares; each square in the sketch is equal to 2" (5 cm). Next, I break down the design into each component (or pattern piece) and determine the size of those as well. Each A pattern piece in Caesar Creek (without its seam allowance) is 8" x 52" (20 cm x 130 cm), which corresponds to the sketch where each A piece measures 4 x 26 squares.

When you are developing patterns and calculating the cutting sizes of each section of the design, it is important to remember to add $\frac{1}{4}$" (6 mm) all around on every pattern piece for the seam allowance. The drawing of the finished design on graph paper does not

include the seam allowance, of course, so it's crucial to remember to add it to your list of the cutting sizes for your pieces; without it, the pieces of the pattern will not fit together properly.

I assign each pattern piece a "name" or label—usually a letter or number, whichever I feel makes the most sense given the overall layout of the design. I record the sizes (which include the seam allowances) of all of the pattern pieces in the sketchbook, either just below the drawing of the design or on the opposite sheet of paper in the book, so that they are close to the sketch.

color

Next, I add color to the design. When I create a color palette, sometimes I am inclined to use colors that are similar to those of the actual object or place that inspired the design, as I did for the Third Street quilt on page 112. Other times, I create a completely new color palette, as I did with my Mason quilt on page 44. Occasionally I use fabric scraps or other ephemera, such as paint chips, as a starting point to determine my color story. I like to look through the colors and combine them with a specific project in mind. Once I've come up with a color scheme, no matter how the colors were chosen, I add those colors into my sketchbook design with marker pens.

I use a few different types of markers, but my favorite ones are Faber-Castell PITT Artist Pens. They contain acid-free India ink, which is a water-based pigment that is typically a dark bluish black, but it also comes in other colors. I prefer these markers because the colors are really beautiful and the ink is translucent, so I can still see my drawn lines and the notated pattern pieces of my sketch, even after it's been colored in. The ink of these markers also doesn't bleed from one page of my sketch to the next, which is important to me. These markers come in a

variety of different sizes and shaped tips, but I prefer to use the PITT Artist Pens with the brush nib that are marked "B" on the cap and barrel of the marker. The brush tip on this style of marker is just the right size for me to be able to neatly color in even small pattern pieces, while giving me the flexibility to fill in large areas of color in bigger pattern pieces as well. I also have a few of the Faber-Castell PITT Big Brush Artist Pens, which, like the name suggests, have a bigger brush tip that allows more ink to be laid down at a time. I think these work better for larger areas of color, but I personally find them a bit too bulky for more detailed work.

fabric

When the drawing for the quilt is complete, with pattern pieces labeled and marked and colors assigned for each component of the quilt, I determine the amount of fabric that will be needed to construct it. I calculate how many pieces I need from each color and use simple math to figure out how much yardage I will need to create each piece in the pattern. The typical width of woven cotton quilting-weight fabric is 44–45" (112–115 cm), and it is safe to estimate a usable width of 42" (106.5 cm) once the narrow, tightly woven selvages on either side of the fabric are excluded. So I add the total number of pieces that I need from each fabric and determine how many yards I will require based on those calculations. I try to be conscientious and create patterns where there is not much wasted fabric, although depending on the design of the quilt, sometimes there are leftovers. This leftover fabric can always be used in other projects. When a quilt calls for a long length of fabric, I usually design the pattern so that the fabric is cut along its length, rather than its width, so that these long pieces are obtained with little or no piecing.

estminster Fibers #LIAB 004 Sky Pyramid ❶○③○○○

I choose the actual fabrics that I want to use to make the quilt based on my colored-in sketch. If I'm looking for a specific shade, I sometimes search through swatch cards of solid fabrics. A swatch card is a chart that contains a swatch of all of the colors that the manufacturer offers the fabric in. Swatch cards of a range of solid-colored fabrics are really handy to have in your sewing area, particularly if you use a lot of solid fabrics like I do. They are available to purchase at some local fabric stores as well as from various online fabric shops. There are so many different colors of solid quilting cottons available now, and these swatch cards make it easy to choose ones to use in a project. I often use the swatch cards in combination with my paint color chips from the hardware store, especially if I'm trying to match a specific color. I will move my paint chip around my various fabric swatch cards until I find one that is the closest match.

If I am using a printed fabric in a project and want to find solids that coordinate with it, I will use the selvage of the print as a starting point. The solid colors that make up the printed design of the fabric are usually included on the selvage, in small circles or other motifs, just after the name of the fabric and its manufacturer. I also use my fabric swatch cards to find solid cottons that coordinate with prints.

Once I have my design, pattern, and fabrics ready for a project, I begin the process of construction, the subject of Chapter 4.

ABOVE Printed fabrics often display the colors that make up the design along the selvage, making it easy to choose coordinating solid fabrics.

chapter 4

BASIC QUILT CONSTRUCTION

I tend to design quilts that are made up of large pattern pieces with simple layouts so they are generally easy to construct, even for beginners. There are many online tutorials available for learning how to sew and quilt. You may also be able to find classes in your area, where you can learn the many skills and techniques for sewing from someone in your community. Although I am completely self-taught, having never taken a sewing class (other than home economics in junior high), I'm a stickler for good construction, including precise cuts of fabrics, even and consistent seam allowances, strong seams, and the like, and these are the skills that I use every day when I'm working on a quilt. The following are my tips for successful basic quilt construction.

PREPARING YOUR QUILT FABRICS

prewashing fabric

Many people prefer to prewash their fabrics before working with them in a sewing or quilting project but I rarely do this for a number of reasons. First of all, it takes a lot of time to wash, dry, and iron fabric, and I'd much rather spend my time creating than doing laundry. The majority of the fabrics that I use are woven 100 percent cotton quilting fabrics, meaning they are created with high-quality dyes and have a high thread count. These cottons only tend to shrink marginally, not enough to concern me.

However, if I am working with another fabric substrate, like linen or vintage fabrics, I will often prewash them to make sure that there is no bleeding of dyes or large amounts of shrinkage. And, especially in the case of vintage fabrics, I want to be sure that the fabric is strong enough.

If a vintage fabric comes out of the wash intact, without falling apart or shredding, I know that it is strong enough to use in a quilt.

When I do prewash a fabric, I typically use a gentle detergent and wash it in cold water and tumble dry on low (the same way I wash and dry my finished quilts). With vintage fabrics, I often also put a color catcher in the wash to catch loose dye. These look like dryer sheets and are sold in the laundry section of most grocery stores.

ironing fabric

It's important to prepare the fabric by ironing it before you cut into it so you can cut accurately shaped pieces. Using a hot iron and a bit of steam, move the iron back and forth over the surface of the fabric until it is free of wrinkles.

OPPOSITE As I cut fabric for a project, I label each piece with masking tape marked with its coordinating pattern-piece name.

CUTTING QUILT TOP PIECES

A table used especially for cutting fabric is nice to have, but certainly not necessary. If you are going to invest in a cutting table, however, you may prefer it to be higher than a standard-sized table. This increase in height of the table will make cutting fabric less strenuous on your back.

When you are ready to cut the fabric, use a large mat specially made for cutting fabrics, a rotary cutter, and a straight-edge plastic ruler. I prefer to use a cutting mat that is at least 24" x 36" (60 cm x 90 cm) in size, but I also have a larger one for bigger jobs that measures 33" x 58" (60 cm x 90 cm). Quilter's cutting mats are marked with a grid made up of 1" (2.5 cm) squares, and fractions—$\frac{1}{4}$", $\frac{1}{2}$", and $\frac{3}{4}$" (6 mm, 12 mm, 2 cm)—are marked along the bottom edge. This grid makes cutting and measuring fabric easy.

To cut fabric, I prefer to use either a 45 mm or a 60 mm rotary cutter because they allow me to cut through multiple layers of fabric at a time, quickly and accurately. Many rotary cutters come with replaceable blades, and it's a good idea to change them frequently. The blades tend to dull quickly, which makes cutting fabric more difficult, and perhaps even more dangerous, as you have to press down harder on the rotary cutter when the blade is dull.

To be safe, rotary cutters should be used in conjunction with a plastic straight edge. I prefer to use a 6" x 24" (15 cm x 60 cm) quilting ruler for most cuts because I think that size is the most versatile for many quilting projects and is easiest to work with. To begin, place the ironed fabric on the cutting mat and smooth out any remaining wrinkles or creases with your hand. Most fabric that is sold in yards (meters), as opposed to smaller cuts, comes folded in half lengthwise (the fold runs parallel to its selvages), which allows for easier handling and cutting. When I am cutting fabric from

selvage to selvage, I first position the fold along the bottom edge of the grid on the cutting mat, then I place the ruler on the fabric where I want to make a cut and carefully run the blade of the rotary cutter along the edge of the plastic ruler, moving it away from me as I make a cut. Make sure your hand is holding the ruler firmly in place and be careful to not cut your fingers with the blade. After you make your cut, replace the safety guide for the rotary cutter to avoid any cutting accidents.

After a strip of fabric is cut from selvage to selvage, I typically subcut that piece into smaller squares, strips, or rectangles, again using the rotary cutter and straight edge in the same manner. I also remove the selvages of the fabric as I'm cutting strips of fabric with my rotary cutter and straight edge. I do not use selvages in the construction of my quilts, as they are more tightly woven, and

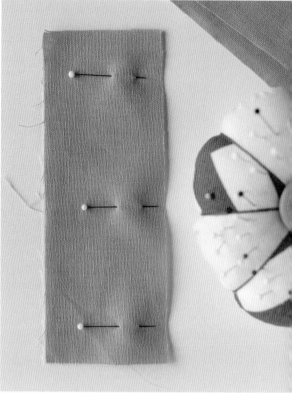

therefore have a different look and feel than the rest of the fabric.

In addition to rotary cutters, I keep designated fabric scissors (never used to cut paper or anything else, which will dull the blades) on hand. I use them for cutting curved pattern pieces, such as the appliqué shapes on the Springfield and Union Terminal quilts (pages 50 and 124) and the circle appliqué shapes on Springfield (page 50). I also have a small pair of scissors that I use for snipping threads.

When I am starting a quilt, I prefer to cut out all of my fabric pieces for the project at one time. Using a marker pen, I write the pattern-piece label on a piece of masking tape—"A," "B," "C," or "D," etc.— and then adhere a tape label to each fabric piece as I cut it out. This keeps everything organized for the subsequent construction of the quilt top. As backup to the adhesive, I often use a sewing pin to pin each tape

label in place on each pattern piece. Once all of the fabric pattern pieces are labeled, I place them in a plastic 15-quart (14-liter) storage bin so they are well organized and easily accessible when needed.

SEWING YOUR QUILT TOP TOGETHER

I do not need a fancy or computerized sewing machine for the type of work I do. In fact, I prefer a non-computerized model because I feel that I have more control over the machine, and therefore my work in general. A basic sewing machine with just a few stitch designs is plenty. I'm much more interested in a machine that is reliable and that has a large throat space. I've recently begun to use a vintage industrial machine for my piecing and construction and I'm really happy with it. It is fast, it produces a beautiful

ABOVE LEFT I store labeled pattern pieces in a plastic bin while I'm working on a project. ABOVE RIGHT When sewing pieces together, align them exactly and pin carefully before stitching.

stitch quality, and it's a workhorse. It also features a built-in table and a large harp area so even large quilting projects are easy to manage.

stitching fabric pieces together

Most fabric has a "right" side and a "wrong" side, and most cut quilt pieces are sewn with right sides together. With printed fabrics, these sides are easy to distinguish because the "right" side is the side that has the printing. Often the printing is still visible from the wrong, or backside, although typically it is much less bright than it appears on the right side.

With solid-colored fabrics, the right and wrong sides are not as easy to distinguish, and honestly, it's not that important. Solid-colored fabrics are typically dyed, instead of printed, and the dyes penetrate both sides of the fiber equally.

When preparing to sew quilt pieces together, I use a lot of pins, placed perpendicularly to the fabric edge, to hold them together. Just remember to remove the pins as you are sewing a seam so you don't stitch over them. It is possible for a pin to break from the force of the sewing machine needle, causing part of the needle and/or pin to break off, fly up, and potentially injure you or anyone else nearby. Alternatively, if I am sewing long strips of fabric together, I'll often place the pins parallel to the edge of the fabrics, about ½" (12 mm) from them, along the length of the fabric. If you choose to pin in this manner, there is no need to remove them as you sew, as they do not get close to the needle during the sewing process. I sew with cotton or cotton/poly blend thread, and I backstitch at the beginning and end of each seam to lock the threads in place and secure each seam.

pressing seams

Once blocks or sections of the quilt top are sewn together, the seams should be pressed as opposed to ironed. When writing about preparing fabric, I mentioned that fabric can be ironed, an act that calls for the hot iron to be moved back and forth across the surface of the fabric. If you were to iron pieced blocks, there would be a chance that you would distort or stretch the fabric by moving the iron back and forth, so it's best to press them instead. Pressing is a technique in which the hot iron is placed on a section of the assembled quilt pieces, but it is not moved back and forth. Instead, it is lifted up completely from the surface of the fabric or quilt top and then moved to a new position and replaced upon it. This technique will ensure that there is little to no shifting of a quilt block that could lead to distortion of the overall design of the quilt top.

FINISHING YOUR QUILT

A quilt, basically speaking, consists of three layers: the quilt top, the middle layer of batting, and the quilt backing. Once the top of the quilt is complete and the quilt backing is pieced together, the next step in the process of construction is to make what is known as a quilt sandwich. I prefer to use a low-loft cotton quilt batting because I like the finish that it creates. Quilts finished with this type of thin batting lay relatively flat when they are washed and dried, though the batting (because it is cotton) shrinks a bit, creating a slightly crinkly surface—a great texture, in my opinion.

basting the layers together

Once you are ready to build your quilt sandwich, place the quilt backing on the floor or on a large table, depending on the

Place quilting pins at regular intervals when basting the quilt layers together.

I like to machine-quilt my work very simply, often with straight lines.

size of your project. The backing should be placed right side down and flat and smooth, so a floor is often the best place for this process. I smooth it out with my hand as I lay it flat on the ground and use pieces of masking tape adhered at various points around the perimeter of the backing to keep it in place.

Next, place the batting on top of the quilt backing, smoothing it out as you go. Another great thing about cotton batting is that it has a tendency to stick to the cotton fabric, which helps adhere it to both the quilt backing and quilt top. Be sure to center the batting on top of the back so that all of it fits within the boundaries of the quilt backing.

Lastly, place the quilt top on the layer of batting, right side up. Again, smooth this layer out as you place it on the batting, making sure to center it as well. Be careful to not pull the quilt top too much or you will run the risk of distorting sections of the piecing.

Once the three layers of the quilt sandwich are in place, use curved quilting pins to baste them together. Basting is a temporary means of holding the layers of fabric and batting together, and in quilting I prefer to use curved quilting pins to do this rather than basting with a needle and thread. These pins are similar to regular safety pins, except one side of them is bent, which makes it easier to push the pin through the layers and back up to the top before closing.

When you are pin-basting, make sure to push the tip of the quilting pin through all three layers and back up again through all three layers. I typically position the pins fairly close together, about 3–4" (9–10 cm) apart. This ensures less shifting of the three layers of the sandwich during the quilting process.

quilting

Most of my work is machine quilted. While I use all-purpose thread for piecing, I like to use a thicker-weight cotton quilting thread for my machine quilting. Quilting is the act of stitching through all three layers of the quilt sandwich. I prefer simple quilting—either straight lines or an allover organic figure-eight—which were used on the quilts in this book. But feel free to experiment with other designs.

Again, there is no need for an expensive sewing machine to obtain beautiful results. You can quilt a straight line design with a basic sewing machine foot, although a walking foot is helpful to have as well. The walking foot is a special foot that attaches to your sewing machine and acts like a feed dog on the top of the layers of fabric, moving them through the throat of the sewing machine as you sew.

For a more organic design, like my freehand figure-eight, you'll need a free-motion quilting foot, which is sometimes referred to as a darning foot. This foot allows you to move the quilt sandwich/layers of fabric in any direction, giving you the freedom to quilt almost any type of design.

If you are quilting on a domestic sewing machine, a pair of quilting gloves can really help maneuver the fabric. I use gloves that have a rubber palm that allows me to hold onto and move the fabric easier than without them. You can purchase these from fabric and quilt shops, but I've also successfully used inexpensive gardening gloves for this purpose.

Many people prefer to have a professional long-arm quilter quilt their projects, instead of finishing them at home on their own sewing machines. Long-arm quilting is the process of sewing through all three layers of a quilt with a long-arm sewing machine, which consists of an industrial sewing machine, a table that measures ten to fourteen feet in length, and several rollers that hold the quilt top, quilt backing, and quilt batting. If you choose to do this, you will only have to construct the quilt front and the quilt back. You will not need to baste them to the batting; the quilter will install the three layers separately on her machine. This type of quilting is usually charged per square inch of design, and the quilter often also supplies the batting for an additional charge. Once the quilting is finished, the long-arm quilter will return the quilt to you, so you can finish it with binding. One thing to keep in mind if you plan on having your project professionally quilted by a long-arm quilter is that the backing of your quilt needs to be about four inches larger than the top of the quilt on each of the four sides, so that the quilter can install it properly on the long-arm machine. I have written all of the patterns for the book with this in mind, so that you can quilt them either way successfully. To locate a professional long-arm quilter, you can search online, or ask your local quilt shop or quilting guilds for local recommendations.

preparing the quilt sandwich for binding

Once the quilting is finished, you must trim off the excess backing fabric and batting with a rotary cutter and a straight edge so that these layers align with the edge of the quilt top.

preparing the binding

The last step in finishing your quilt is binding the outer edge. I make my binding out of fabric strips 2½" (6 cm) wide, and I've specified in the instructions the number of fabric strips that are required for each design in the book. To create the continuous binding strip, sew the cut strips together end-to-end. This can be done by sewing the straight ends together, or to reduce bulk—and the way I prefer to do it—by sewing them together with a diagonal seam, rather than a straight seam.

FIG. 1. When sewing binding strips together end-to-end, use diagonal seams to reduce bulk.

FIG. 2. Press a diagonal fold into the beginning of the binding strip as a guideline for the final binding seam.

FIG. 3. Sew the folded binding as a double layer to the quilt edge, with all raw edges aligned.

FIG. 4. At each corner, backstitch to lock the stitches and then remove the quilt from the machine.

FIG. 5. Fold the binding up at the corner to form a diagonal 45-degree fold and finger press the fold.

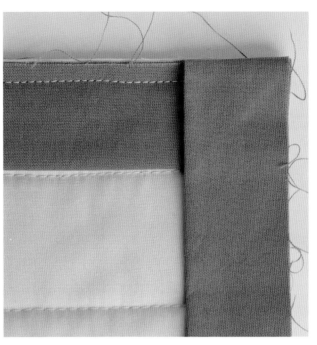

FIG. 6. Fold the binding back down over the diagonal fold and align it with the next side edge of the quilt.

For a diagonal seam, place one strip on top of the other, laying the top piece perpendicular to the bottom, and extending each strip approximately ¼" (6 mm) over each other. To ensure an accurate seam, use a pencil and a ruler to draw a straight line between the points where the bottom strip meets the top strip. Pin the strips in place with two pins and sew a seam along the pencil line, backstitching at the beginning and end of the seam for reinforcement (Fig. 1, opposite).

Trim off the excess fabric, leaving a ¼" (6 mm) seam allowance, and press the seam open with a hot iron. Repeat this process until all the strips are sewn together. Using a hot iron, press the pieced binding in half lengthwise with wrong sides together, so that the folded strip is approximately 1¼" (3 cm) wide. Once the binding has been pressed, open about 3" (7.5 cm) of one end and make a diagonal fold in the strip by bringing the wrong sides together, about 1½" (4 cm) from the end (Fig. 2). Press the fold with a hot iron. Keep the remainder of the binding folded in half lengthwise because it is stitched to the quilt as a double layer.

sewing on the binding

At this stage, fold the binding over itself to create a neat pile, instead of a long and lengthy mess of fabric. It is easier to handle and attach this way. Move the quilt to the sewing machine, with the backing facing up, to prepare to sew the binding. Starting in the middle of one side, lay the binding on the quilt backing, lining up both raw edges of the binding with the raw edges of the quilt. Then begin to sew the binding in place about 5" (13 cm) from the diagonal fold at the beginning of binding, using a ¼" (6 mm) seam allowance (Fig. 3).

FIG. 7. Keeping the corner folded, start again at the corner and continue sewing on the binding along the next side edge.

FIG. 8. Once you have sewn the ends of the binding together with a diagonal seam, trim the seam and press it open.

FIG. 9. Press the folded edge of the binding onto the right side of the quilt. At each corner press a diagonal fold for a miter.

Continue sewing toward the corner and stop when you are about ¼" (6 mm) away from the next side of the quilt (Fig. 4). Backstitch to lock the stitches and then snip the threads and remove the quilt from the sewing machine. At the corner, fold the binding up toward the side you just sewed on, perpendicularly on top of itself, making a 45-degree angle (Fig. 5). Press it in place with your finger and then bring it back down on itself along the edge of the next side of the quilt to create a mitered corner (Fig. 6).

Bring the quilt back to the sewing machine, pivot it, and continue to sew the binding on in the same manner along the next side (Fig. 7). When you get to the corner, treat it like you did at the last corner.

Once you've reached the side of the quilt you started on, stop sewing about 12" (30 cm) away from the place where you started the binding and take the quilt out of the machine. Open out the pressed and unsewn end of binding that you just stopped stitching on and pin a single edge in place along the edge of the quilt until it nearly reaches the beginning section of the binding. Next, lay the beginning end of the binding with the diagonal fold on top of the section you just pinned in place, pull taut and pin in place. Using a water-soluble pen, mark a line on the binding underneath along the edge of the diagonal fold at the beginning of the binding. Unpin the binding and line up the two ends so that they're perpendicular to each other, just as when you constructed the binding from the individual strips of fabric. Pin the two sides together, placing the diagonal crease on the top piece directly over the line on the bottom piece that you just marked. Using the fold on the fabric as a guide, sew a seam and backstitch at the beginning and end. Remove the quilt from the sewing machine and lay the unsewn section of binding along the edge of the quilt to check that it is the proper length needed to finish, before trimming any of the excess binding away. If it fits correctly, pick up the unsewn section of the binding and trim off the excess fabric, leaving a $\frac{1}{4}$" (6 mm) seam allowance. Press the seam open (Fig. 8).

Fold the unsewn section of binding in half and press with a hot iron. Pin this unsewn section of binding in place along the back of the quilt and sew with a $\frac{1}{4}$" (6 mm) seam allowance, backstitching at the beginning and end of the seam to finish.

As an optional step, I use a serger to overstitch the raw edges of the quilt and binding. There are a lot of loose threads along these raw edges and by running them through a serger, everything is kept nice and tidy. If you don't have a serger, you could also sew a zigzag stitch along the edges to keep them tidy and cover up any loose threads.

To complete the binding, first turn the quilt over so that the top side is up and pull the binding up from the back so that it lays flat, extending beyond the edge of the quilt. Fold the binding down over the raw edge of the quilt and press in place with a hot iron (Fig. 9). Next, pin the binding in position, placing the pins through both the binding and the quilt and keeping them parallel to the edge of the quilt.

As an alternative to holding the binding in place with pins at this stage, I sometimes use a thin line of white school glue to temporarily hold the binding in place. Just run a small amount of glue along the inside edge of the binding, fold it over and press with a hot iron to hold it in place. I like this method because it produces a neat finished edge on my quilts and I don't run the risk of poking myself with a lot of pins, as is often the case with the former method.

To create a mitered corner, fold the edge of the binding so that it creates a 45-degree angle and press with a hot iron. Pull the binding on the other side of the corner taut and press with a hot iron. Fold the corner over and pin it in place.

Once the binding has been pinned or glued down, move the quilt to the sewing machine and topstitch just along the edge of the binding. If you used pins to hold the binding in place, remove them as you sew. When you meet a corner, sew just until you reach the fold in the binding, and then sew a few stitches along the edge of the fold itself to tack it down and hold it in place. Then backstitch along the fold and continue to sew along the edge of the binding on the next side of the quilt. Sew along the entire perimeter of the quilt until the binding is attached on all sides, and backstitch to secure the seam at the end to finish.

PART 2 QUILTS

lebanon

This design came to me when I was looking at the windows of the Citizens National Bank in Lebanon, Ohio. The building was built in 1908 and is a beautiful marble-faced structure that takes up almost an entire block. I was captivated by the banks of windows on the second floor, particularly by the groupings of three with the decorative architectural elements above each set. In my design I focused on those square architectural elements, recreating them in patchwork blocks and placing them on a lower plane of the design, beneath a large area of negative space. While I tend to choose simple quilting for all of my own personal projects, this expansive area of negative space (background) would be a great place for more complex and varied free-motion quilting patterns. Feel free to experiment.

I used a simple color palette of just two hues for my first version of the quilt—a light dusty blue and light oyster white—to replicate the actual colors of the building. The colors are similar in value, both being mid-tone hues, and this is one of my favorite palettes to work with because I think the overall look is sophisticated and very soothing. The color temperature of this palette is cool, as both the muted blue and the neutral are cool colors.

For the printed fabric in the patchwork squares of the second version, I chose a pink, coral, and cream large-scale paisley design. I combined this patterned fabric with a solid hot pink cotton, pulling that color from one that appears in the print itself. Since the patchwork squares are made up of many colors in this version, they don't pop as much as they do in the first version, where they are made of one solid color. This color palette is much warmer in temperature than that of the first version.

FINISHED QUILT SIZE
50½" x 66½" (126.2 cm x 166.2 cm)

FABRICS
The fabric amounts are based on using 44-45" (112-115 cm) wide fabrics.

COLORWAY 1
BLUE AND BEIGE

FABRIC 1: 3 yards (2.7 m) of a solid light blue, such as Robert Kaufman *Kona Cotton Solids* in Dusty Blue (362)

FABRIC 2: ½ yard (50 cm) of a solid light beige, such as Robert Kaufman *Kona Cotton Solids* in Bone (1037)

BACKING FABRIC: 3½ yards (3.2 m) of desired fabric

BINDING FABRIC: ½ yard (50 cm) more of Fabric 1

COLORWAY 2
PINK AND RED

FABRIC 1: 3 yards (2.7 m) of a solid hot pink, such as FreeSpirit *Designer Solids* in Cotton Candy (S57)

FABRIC 2: ½ yard (50 cm) of a red, pink, and white small-scale print, such as FreeSpirit *Alchemy Organic – Flora* by Amy Butler in Coral

BACKING FABRIC: 3½ yards (3.2 m) of desired fabric

BINDING FABRIC: ½ yard (50 cm) more of Fabric 1

OTHER MATERIALS
+ 55" x 71" (137 cm x 177 cm) piece of batting (or a twin-sized package)

+ All-purpose thread for piecing

+ Off-white quilting thread for colorway 1, OR light pink for colorway 2

CUT THE QUILT-TOP PIECES

1 Using a rotary cutter, straight edge, and a cutting mat, cut a 50½" (126.2 cm) x width of fabric (WOF) piece from Fabric 1, cutting from selvage to selvage. Then trim this piece of fabric into one 40½" x 50½" (101.2 cm x 126.2 cm) rectangle for the A piece (the solid top section of the quilt). Pin a label to your pieces as you cut them.

2 From Fabric 1, cut another 50½" (126.2 cm) x WOF piece. Then subcut this piece *lengthwise* into one 12½" x 50½" (31.2 cm x 126.2 cm) strip for the K piece (the solid bottom section of the quilt), three 2½" x 50½" (6.2 cm x 126.2 cm) strips, one 6½" x 50½" (16.2 cm x 126.2 cm) strip, and two 1½" x 50½" strips (3.7 cm x 126.2 cm). Set the K piece aside with the A piece.

3 Take the three 2½" (6.2 cm) Fabric 1 strips and subcut them into four 2½" x 4½" (6.2 cm x 11.2 cm) strips for four B pieces, ten 2½" x 6½" (6.2 cm x 16.2 cm) strips for ten C pieces, and eight 2½" x 2½" (6.2 cm x 6.2 cm) squares for eight E pieces. Remember to label your pieces as you cut them.

4 Take the 6½" x 50½" (16.2 cm x 126.2 cm) Fabric 1 strip and subcut it into two 4½" x 6½" (11.2 cm x 16.2 cm) rectangles for two H pieces, and five 6½" x 6½" (16.2 cm x 16.2 cm) squares for five J pieces.

5 Trim the two 1½" x 50½" (3.7 cm x 126.2 cm) Fabric 1 strips so they each measure 1½" x 42" (3.7 cm x 105 cm). Set them aside to be used in step 8 to make the D blocks.

6 From Fabric 2, cut three 2½" (6.2 cm) x WOF strips. Subcut these strips into six 2½" x 10½" (6.2 cm x 26.2 cm) strips for six F pieces, and six 2½" x 6½" (6.2 cm x 16.2 cm) strips for six G pieces.

7 From Fabric 2, cut two 1½" (3.7 cm) x WOF strips. Then trim these two strips so they are each 42" (105 cm) long. These will be used in step 8 to make the D blocks.

CONSTRUCT THE D BLOCKS

8 With right sides together and using a ¼" (6 mm) seam allowance for all seams, sew one 1½" x 42" (3.7 cm x 105 cm) strip of Fabric 1 to one 1½" x 42" (3.7 cm x 105 cm) strip of Fabric 2, stitching along the length of the strips. Press the seam allowances to the side, toward the darker fabric. Repeat with the remaining 1½" (3.7 cm) strips of Fabric 1 and Fabric 2.

9 Cut each of the two pieced strips into twelve 2½" x 2½" (6.2 cm x 6.2 cm) squares for a total of 24 D blocks.

CONSTRUCT THE QUILT TOP

10 Start constructing the quilt top by sewing together the rows that make up the pieced section. Construct row 1 first, using two B strips, five C strips, and six D blocks. Following the diagram and using a ¼" (6 mm) seam allowance for all seams, sew one B piece to one D block, with the D block positioned as shown. Sew one C strip to the other side of the D block. Continue adding on a D block and a C strip alternately, until all five C strips have been added. Finish by sewing on the sixth D block and the remaining B strip. This completes row 1. Press all seams to the side, toward the darker fabric.

9 *Cutting D blocks from the pieced strip.*

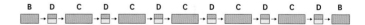

10 *Sewing together row 1.*

11 For row 2, use six D blocks, four E squares, and three F strips. Following the diagram, sew one E square to one D block, with the D block positioned as shown. Sew one F strip to the other side of the D block. Then add on one D square, followed by one E square and one D block. Continuing in this sequence, sew on one F strip, followed by one D block, one E square, and one D block. Sew on the last F strip, followed by the last D block and the last E square. This completes row 2. Press all seams to the side, toward the dark fabric, except the seams between the D blocks and the F pieces, where you should press the seams toward the F piece.

12 For row 3, use six G strips, two H pieces, and five J squares. Following the diagram, sew one H piece to one G strip. Sew one J square to the other side of the G strip. Continue in this way, adding on one G strip and one J square alternately until one G strip and one H piece remain. Then sew on the last G strip, followed by the last H piece. This completes row 3. Press all seams to the side, toward the dark fabric.

13 Construct row 4 as for row 2 in step 11.

14 Construct row 5 as for row 1 in step 10, orienting the D blocks as shown.

15 Following the diagram, sew the rows together while carefully aligning the seams of the various pieces. First, sew row 1 to row 2, so that the Fabric 2 section of the D blocks touch the F strips in Fabric 2. Sew row 3 to the bottom of row 2, and then row 4 to the bottom of row 3. Sew row 5 to the bottom of row 4, so that the Fabric 2 section of the D blocks touch the F strips in Fabric 2. Press all seams toward the side.

16 Sew the A piece to the top of the pieced rows and the K piece to the bottom of the pieced rows to complete the quilt top. Press the seams to the side.

11 *Sewing together row 2.*

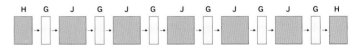

12 *Sewing together row 3.*

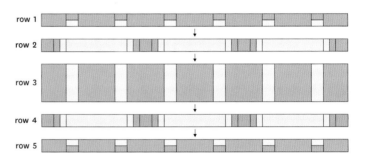

15 *Sewing rows 1–5 together.*

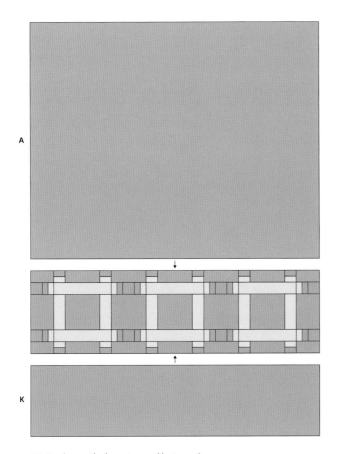

16 *Sewing on the large top and bottom pieces.*

17 To make the quilt back, cut two 58" (147 cm) x WOF pieces out of the backing fabric. Trimming off the selvages as you do so, trim each piece *lengthwise* so that it measures 37½" x 58" (95 cm x 147 cm). Sew the pieces right sides together, along one long edge, and press the the seam allowances to the side.

FINISH THE QUILT

18 Layer the quilt top, batting, and quilt back to make a quilt sandwich (page 29). Baste together with quilting pins or basting stitches (page 30).

19 Quilt as desired (page 31). After quilting, trim off the excess batting and backing fabric to align them with the edges of the quilt top, and square up all sides of the quilt if necessary.

20 From the binding fabric, cut six 2½" (6 cm) x WOF strips. Cut off the selvages and sew the six strips together end-to-end to create the continuous binding strip (page 31). Bind the quilt as desired (page 33).

mason

This is sort of the project that started it all, or at least my work that deals with designs that are inspired by non-traditional places and locations. The design for Mason was inspired by a painted grid in the parking lot of a local big box store. One day as my family and I arrived there, I noticed the graphic quality of those painted lines and snapped a quick photo on my phone. Back at my studio, after a few tweaks in my sketchbook, I came up with this quilt.

Both versions are made of four solid-colored cottons. In the first version, the main color is a dark rich taupe, which acts as a neutral in this palette. I've contrasted the neutral with brighter saturated colors, mainly a bright robin's egg blue and pops of lime green and orange. I think this palette works well because the neutral tone of the taupe balances the other bright colors, so they don't feel overwhelming but still retain a rich impact.

The second version contains more muted colors. I've replaced the taupe background of the first version with an off-white background and used a jade green for the main linear "framework" of the patchwork. The dark gray rectangles on either side of the lighter green squares in the center really draw your eye to the middle of the design and create a lot of optical movement across the surface of the arrangement. Enhancing this movement is the stark contrast between the cream color and the patchwork strips in the center of the quilt.

FINISHED QUILT SIZE
60½" x 68½" (151.5 cm x 171.5 cm)

FABRICS
The fabric amounts are based on using 44–45" (112–115 cm) wide fabrics.

COLORWAY 1
TAUPE, TURQUOISE, GREEN, AND PUMPKIN

FABRIC 1: 3 yards (2.8 m) of a solid taupe, such as Moda *Bella Solids* in Weathered Teak (129)

FABRIC 2: 1½ yards (1.4 m) of a solid turquoise, such as Moda *Bella Solids* in Robin's Egg Blue (85)

FABRIC 3: ¼ yard (25 cm) of a solid light green, such as Moda *Bella Solids* in Pistachio (134)

FABRIC 4: ¼ yard (25 cm) of a solid pumpkin, such as Moda *Bella Solids* in Orange (80)

BACKING FABRIC: 4 yards (3.7 m) of desired fabric

BINDING FABRIC: ½ yard (50 cm) more of Fabric 3

COLORWAY 2
WHITE, SEA GREEN, CHARCOAL, AND LIGHT GREEN

FABRIC 1: 3 yards (2.8 m) of a solid off-white, such as FreeSpirit *Designer Solids* in Natural (S44)

FABRIC 2: 1½ yards (1.4 m) of a solid sea green, such as Moda *Bella Solids* in Jade (108)

FABRIC 3: ¼ yard (25 cm) of a solid charcoal, such as Robert Kaufman *Kona Cotton Solids* in Charcoal (1071)

FABRIC 4: ¼ yard (25 cm) of a solid light green, such as Robert Kaufman *Kona Cotton Solids* in Olive (1263)

BACKING FABRIC: 4 yards (3.7 m) of desired fabric

BINDING FABRIC: ½ yard (50 cm) more of Fabric 1

OTHER MATERIALS
+ 65" x 73" (162 cm x 182 cm) piece of batting (or a twin-sized package)

+ All-purpose thread for piecing

+ Taupe quilting thread for colorway 1, OR off-white for colorway 2

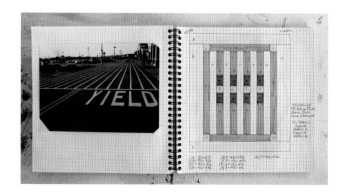

CUT THE QUILT-TOP PIECES

1 Using a rotary cutter, straight edge, and a cutting mat, cut a 60½" (151.2 cm) x width of fabric (WOF) piece of Fabric 1, cutting from selvage to selvage. Subcut this piece *lengthwise* into four 8½" x 60½" (21.2 cm x 151.2 cm) strips. Keep two strips measuring 8½" x 60½" (21.2 cm x 151.2 cm) for two A pieces, and trim the other two strips to 8½" x 52½" (21.2 cm x 131.2 cm) for two B pieces. Pin a label to your pieces as you cut them.

2 From Fabric 1, cut a 44½" (111.2 cm) x WOF piece of fabric. Subcut this piece *lengthwise* into five 4½" x 44½" (11.2 cm x 111.2 cm) strips for five F pieces.

3 From Fabric 2, cut a 44½" (111.2 cm) x WOF piece of fabric. Subcut this piece *lengthwise* into seven 4½" x 44½" (11.2 cm x 111.2 cm) strips. Keep two strips measuring 4½" x 44½" (11.2 cm x 111.2 cm) for two E pieces, and trim two other strips to 4½" x 36½" (11.2 cm x 91.2 cm) for two D pieces. From the remaining three strips, cut eight 4½" x 14½" (11.2 cm x 36.2 cm) strips for eight G pieces.

4 From Fabric 3, cut a 6½" (16.2 cm) x WOF strip of fabric. Subcut this strip into eight 4½" x 6½" (11.2 cm x 16.2 cm) rectangles for eight H pieces.

5 From Fabric 4, cut a 4½" (11.2 cm) x WOF strip of fabric. Subcut this strip into eight 4½" x 4½" (11.2 cm x 11.2 cm) squares for four C pieces and four J pieces.

CONSTRUCT THE QUILT TOP

6 Following the diagram, construct the four pieced columns. Each column is made up of two G pieces, two H pieces, and one J square. With right sides together and using a ¼" (6 mm) seam allowance for all seams, sew the five pieces together end-to-end in this order—G, H, J, H, G. Make a total of four pieced columns in this way. Press all seams to the side.

7 Next, construct the quilt center. It is made up of two E strips, five F strips, and the four pieced columns. Sew the strips and columns together in the order shown in the diagram. Press all seams to the side and set the quilt center aside.

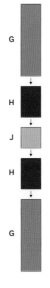

6 *Sewing together the pieced columns.*

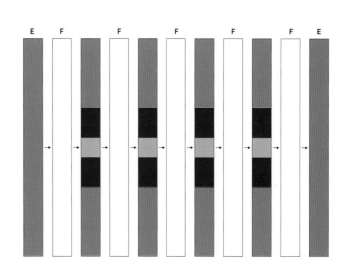

7 *Sewing together the quilt center.*

8 Following the diagram, sew one C square to each end of one D strip. Do the same with the two remaining C squares and the one remaining D strip. Press all seams to the side.

9 Following the diagram, sew one C-D pieced row to the top of the quilt center and one to the bottom. Press all seams to the side.

10 Sew one B strip to the left side of the quilt center and one to the right side. Then sew one A strip to the top of the quilt and one to the bottom. Press all seams to the side.

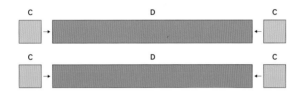

8 *Sewing together the C squares and D strips.*

CUT AND PIECE THE QUILT BACK

11 To make the quilt back, cut two 68" (173 cm) x WOF pieces out of the backing fabric. Trimming off the selvages as you do so, trim each piece *lengthwise* so that it measures 38½" x 68" (98 cm x 173 cm). Sew the pieces right sides together, along one long edge, and press the seam allowances to the side.

FINISH THE QUILT

12 Layer the quilt top, batting, and quilt back to make a quilt sandwich (page 29). Baste together with quilting pins or basting stitches (page 30).

13 Quilt as desired (page 31). After quilting, trim off the excess batting and backing fabric to align them with the edges of the quilt top, and square up all sides of the quilt if necessary.

14 From the binding fabric, cut seven 2½" (6 cm) x WOF strips. Cut off the selvages and sew the seven strips together end-to-end to create the continuous binding strip (page 31). Bind the quilt as desired (page 33).

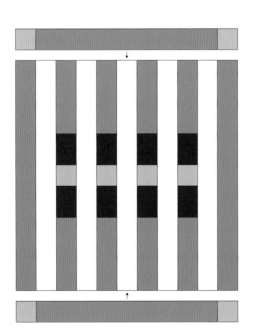

9 *Sewing the C-D pieced rows to the quilt center.*

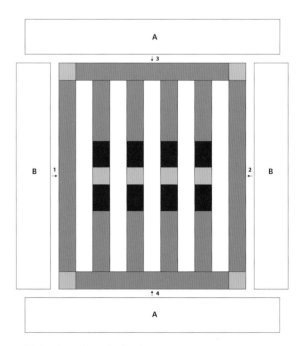

10 *Sewing on the outer borders.*

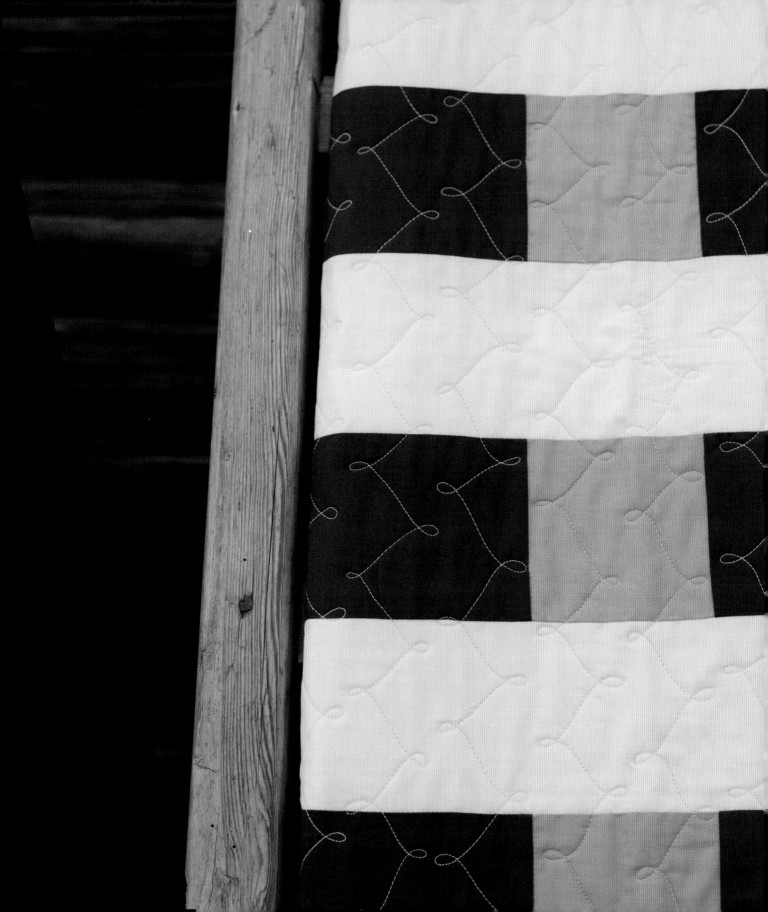

springfield

A metal grate that I bought at a large antiques fair in Springfield, Ohio, gave me the crisp graphic layout for this small quilt, which makes a great wall hanging or table topper. I'm not quite sure of the original use of the grate, although I suspect it may have been part of an industrial fan or air circulation system. The modern look of this quilt reminds me of those great atomic designs of mid-twentieth-century objects.

Even though this quilt design appears complex, it's easy to construct. The circles are hand-cut and then appliquéd onto the background with fusible adhesive webbing, eliminating most of the sewing other than the quilting and the binding. While there are a total of 109 circles, hand-cutting them isn't difficult—I cut mine while relaxing in front of the television.

The color palette of the first version comes from the source inspiration. The solid gray cotton echoes the metal, and the creamy white circles recreate the look of the negative space of the circles. For the second version, I chose a small-scale geometric print in shades of black and white and a solid black cotton so that there is less difference in value between the circles and the background.

Although the adhesive that holds the circles in place is relatively strong, this quilt is not meant for heavy use. If you want to make it more durable, you could stitch around the perimeter of each circle after it is fused in place, either with a straight stitch or a zigzag stitch.

FINISHED QUILT SIZE
22½" x 22½" (53.4 cm x 53.4 cm)

FABRICS
The fabric amounts are based on using 44–45" (112–115 cm) wide fabrics.

COLORWAY 1
GRAY AND OFF-WHITE

FABRIC 1: ¾ yard (70 cm) of a solid gray, such as FreeSpirit *Designer Solids* in Nugray (S98)

FABRIC 2: ½ yard (50 cm) of a solid off-white, such as Robert Kaufman *Kona Cotton Solids* in Snow (1339)

BACKING FABRIC: ¾ yard (70 cm) more of Fabric 1

BINDING FABRIC: ¼ yard (25 cm) more of Fabric 1

COLORWAY 2
GRAY AND BLACK

FABRIC 1: ¾ yard (70 cm) of a charcoal gray print, such as FreeSpirit *Curious Nature – Universe* by David Butler in Night

FABRIC 2: ⅓ yard (35 cm) of a solid black, such as Robert Kaufman *Kona Cotton Solids* in Black (1019)

BACKING FABRIC: ¾ yard (70 cm) more of Fabric 1

BINDING FABRIC: ¼ yard (25 cm) more of Fabric 1

OTHER MATERIALS

+ Large sheet of paper, for the layout template

+ ½ yard (50 cm) of a heavy-duty iron-on paper-backed fusible adhesive webbing, 17" (43 cm) wide—I used 17" (43 cm) wide Pellon® *Heavy-Duty Wonder Under*

+ 25" x 25" (63.5 cm x 63.5 cm) piece of batting

+ All-purpose thread

+ Light gray quilting thread for both colorways

+ 13 sandwich-size zip-able clear plastic bags (optional)

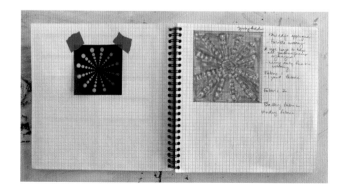

CUT THE QUILT-TOP PIECES

1   Using a rotary cutter, straight edge, and a cutting mat, cut one 22½" (57 cm) x width of fabric (WOF) piece from Fabric 1, cutting from selvage to selvage. Remove the selvages and trim the piece to a 22½" x 22½" (57 cm x 57 cm) square for the quilt top.

2   From Fabric 2, cut one 17½" (44.5 cm) x WOF strip. Remove the selvages and trim the piece to a 17½" x 18½" (44.5 cm x 47 cm) rectangle.

3   Cut the fusible webbing to a 17" x 18" (43 cm x 45.7 cm) rectangle—this is so that it will fit onto the piece of Fabric 2 with ¼" (6mm) extra of fabric all around. Trace 12 sets of the circle templates (on page 156) onto the paper backing of the fusible webbing. Label each circle 1–9, as indicated on the circles template.

4   Trace the center circle template on the paper backing of the fusible webbing.

5   Following the manufacturer's instructions, adhere the fusible webbing to the wrong side of the Fabric 2 piece.

6   Cut out all 109 circles with a pair of scissors. To keep the circles organized, place each of the 12 sets of nine circles in a small zipped plastic bag. Place the center circle in a separate bag so you don't misplace it.

MAKE THE LAYOUT TEMPLATE

7   Using a large sheet of paper at least 24" (61 cm) square, draw a square 22½" x 22½" (57 cm x 57 cm) in the center of the sheet of paper. Draw a line vertically through the center of the drawn square and then horizontally through the center of it to divide it into equal quarters. Enlarge the circles layout template on page 157 as instructed. Then using the template, draw the circles layout in each quarter of the drawn square, aligning the center point of the template with the center on the large drawn square.

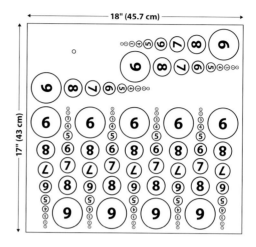

3   Tracing the circles onto the fusible webbing.

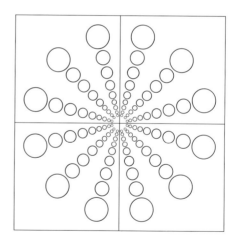

7   Drawing the layout template.

CONSTRUCT THE QUILT TOP

8   Mark the quilt top into quarters with creases. To do this, fold the 22½" (57 cm) Fabric 1 square in half lengthwise, right sides together, and press in the fold with a hot iron. Then open out the fabric, fold in half widthwise, right sides together, and press in this fold. The center is now marked where the creases intersect.

9   Tape the paper layout template to a large window. With the right side facing outward, tape the Fabric 1 square to the template, aligning the fabric creases and the center point with the lines on the template. Lightly trace each circle onto the right side of the fabric with a pencil.

10 Take the Fabric 1 square from the window and move it back to the ironing board. Remove the backing from the center circle, place it at the center crease line of the quilt top, and iron it in place, following the manufacturer's instructions for the webbing.

11 Now you are ready to add the sets of circles. Remove the paper backing from one set of nine circles and position them on the quilt top, along one line of nine circles drawn on the fabric top. Fuse these nine circles in place. Repeat with each set of nine circles until all of the sets of circles are fused to the quilt top. Then fuse on the center circle.

CUT THE QUILT BACK

12 For the quilt back, cut one 27" x 27" (70 cm x 70 cm) square out of the backing fabric.

FINISH THE QUILT

13 Layer the quilt top, batting, and quilt back to make a quilt sandwich (page 29). Baste together with quilting pins or basting stitches (page 30).

14 Quilt as desired (page 31). After quilting, trim off the excess batting and backing fabric to align them with the edges of the quilt top, and square up all sides of the quilt if necessary.

15 From the binding fabric, cut three 2½" (6 cm) x WOF strips. Cut off the selvages and sew the three strips together end-to-end to create the continuous binding (page 31). Bind the quilt as desired (page 33).

kent

I found my inspiration for Kent in a very mundane and unlikely place: the bathroom of a fast-food restaurant. When I entered I was struck by the beauty of the tile that lined the walls. The repetition of thin lines in shades of black, gray, and white in seemingly random order caught my imagination.

Kent is composed of thin fabric strips arranged in random order so that each maker will naturally create a unique design. I made my first version with four solid-colored cotton fabrics in a neutral palette very similar to the inspiration. For the second color scheme, I used shades of pink, cranberry red, black, and creamy white. I especially like how the large-scale floral prints in this version change when cut into small strips and then again when pieced back together in the patchwork of the design. Like the first version, there is not a lot of variation of color here, but adding prints creates more visual interest and movement throughout the composition.

FINISHED QUILT SIZE
60" x 70½" (152.5 cm x 176 cm)

FABRICS
The fabric amounts are based on using 44–45" (112–115 cm) wide fabrics.

COLORWAY 1
BLACK, GRAYS, AND OFF-WHITE

FABRIC 1: 1½ yards (1.4 m) of a solid black, such as Robert Kaufman *Kona Cotton Solids* in Pepper (359)

FABRIC 2: 1½ yards (1.4 m) of a solid charcoal, such as Robert Kaufman *Kona Cotton Solids* in Charcoal (1071)

FABRIC 3: 1½ yards (1.4 m) of a solid light gray, such as Robert Kaufman *Kona Cotton Solids* in Ash (1007)

FABRIC 4: 1½ yards (1.4 m) of a solid off-white, such as Robert Kaufman *Kona Cotton Solids* in Snow (1339)

BACKING FABRIC: 4 yards (3.7 m) of desired fabric

BINDING FABRIC: ½ yard (50 cm) more of Fabric 1

COLORWAY 2
WHITE, CRANBERRY, AND BLACK

FABRIC 1: 1½ yards (1.4 m) of a large-scale floral print, such as FreeSpirit *Greenfield Hill— Preservation Peony* by Denyse Schmidt in Cranberry

FABRIC 2: 1½ yards (1.4 m) of a black, coral, and white small-scale swirl print, such as FreeSpirit *Greenfield Hill—Miss Eleanor* by Denyse Schmidt in Cranberry

FABRIC 3: 1½ yards (1.4 m) of a black and coral plaid, such as FreeSpirit *Greenfield Hill— Griswold Plaid* by Denyse Schmidt in Cranberry

FABRIC 4: 1½ yards (1.4 m) of a coral and white stripe with black dots, such as FreeSpirit *Greenfield Hill—Library Stripe* by Denyse Schmidt in Cranberry

BACKING FABRIC: 4 yards (3.7 m) of desired fabric

BINDING FABRIC: ½ yard (50 cm) of a solid black, such as Robert Kaufman *Kona Cotton Solids* in Pepper (359)

OTHER MATERIALS
+ 64" x 75" (163 cm x 186 cm) piece of batting (or a twin-sized package)

+ All-purpose thread for piecing

+ Light gray quilting thread for colorway 1, OR light pink for colorway 2

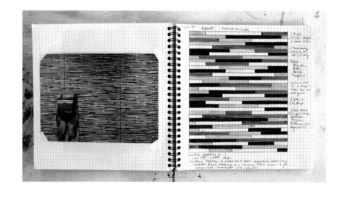

CUT THE QUILT-TOP PIECES

1   Using a rotary cutter, straight edge, and a cutting mat, cut all 1½ yards (1.4 m) of Fabric 1 into 36 strips, each 1½" (3.7 cm) x width of fabric (WOF), cutting from selvage to selvage. Trim off the selvages.

2   Repeat step 1 with Fabrics 2, 3, and 4. Cutting 36 strips in each fabric allows for more strips than you will need for the top, but it gives you more design flexibility when piecing the strips. If you want to be more economical with your fabric, cut 30 strips in each fabric to start, and cut more only as you need them.

CONSTRUCT THE PIECED STRIPS

3   Using two (or three) of the 1½" (3.7 cm) strips in two (or three) different fabrics, construct a pieced strip that measures at least 61" (155 cm) in length. Use pieces of random lengths for the pieced strip. When you are satisfied with the design of the pieced strip, stitch the pieces together end-to-end, using a ¼" (6 mm) seam allowance for all seams. Press the seams open. Trim the pieced strip so that it measures 61" (155 cm) long.

4   Repeat step 3 to make a total of 70 randomly pieced strips, each 61" (155 cm) long. Sew the strip pieces together in random order, making sure to vary the colors and color positions, and strip piece lengths, to give the design more interest. As you construct more pieced strips, you'll have more odd strip lengths that can be used to sew more strips.

3   *Making the first pieced strip.*

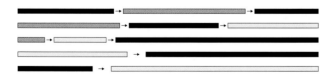

4   *Making the remaining randomly pieced strips.*

CONSTRUCT THE QUILT TOP

5   Lay out the pieced strips on the floor or design wall to create a layout that you like.

6   Begin to construct the quilt top by piecing the strips together in pairs. Place the first two strips with right sides together and stitch together along one long edge, using a ¼" (6 mm) seam allowance. Keeping your layout correct, repeat with the remaining 68 strips to make a total of 35 two-strip sets. Press the seams open as you proceed.

7   Sew three two-strip sets together to create a six-strip set.

8   Repeat step 7 ten times, then sew the remaining two two-strip sets together to make a total of 11 six-strip sets and one four-strip set.

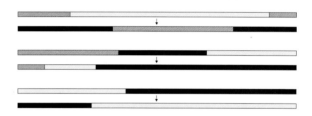

6   *Sewing the strips together in pairs.*

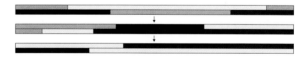

7   *Sewing three two-strip sets together.*

9 *Sewing the six-strip sets together in pairs.*

11 *Completing the quilt top.*

9   Sew two six-strip sections together, following your layout.

10 Repeat step 9 five times, then sew the remaining six-strip set and four-strip set together. You will now have five twelve-strip sets and one ten-strip set.

11 Sew each of the six strip sets together, following your layout, to complete the quilt top. Trim both side edges of the quilt to square them up and to make the quilt top 60" (152.5 cm) wide.

CUT AND PIECE THE QUILT BACK

12 To make the quilt back, cut two 68" (173 cm) x WOF pieces out of the backing fabric. Trim the selvages off of each piece. Sew the pieces right sides together, along one long edge, and press the seam allowances to the side. Trim the backing to 66" x 77" (168 cm x 191 cm).

FINISH THE QUILT

13 Layer the quilt top, batting, and quilt back to make a quilt sandwich (page 29). Baste together with quilting pins or basting stitches (page 30).

14 Quilt as desired (page 31). After quilting, trim off the excess batting and backing fabric to align them with the edges of the quilt top, and square up all sides of the quilt if necessary.

15 From the binding fabric, cut seven 2½" (6 cm) x WOF strips. Cut off the selvages and sew the seven strips together end-to-end to create the continuous binding strip (page 31). Bind the quilt as desired (page 33).

maineville

The hen house at a local farm owned by a friend of my family inspired my Maineville quilt. I was first drawn to the linear design of the old wooden slats and the repetition of horizontal elements. Upon further study I noticed the section along the roofline where the joist beams create a secondary pattern of rectangles, breaking up the horizontal lines of the slats, and I decided to focus on those elements for the quilt. Instead of keeping each horizontal band of the quilt the same width, as they are in the barn, I varied them to add motion to the design. I also replaced the rectangles of the joists with squares in my quilt.

For the first version of the quilt, I chose fabrics that are similar in color to the weathered wood of the barn and the red metal roof of the building behind it, namely pale gray and creamy white, with a coral red accent in the large squares. The overall palette is neutral due to the large area of cream and gray, while the saturated coral-red adds intensity and draws the eye to the upper portion of the work.

In the second version I replaced the solid coral-red with a small-scale geometric print for the square blocks, and I chose two solid-colored cotton fabrics that coordinate with the print for the wide stripes. I selected darker colors for these, replacing the pale gray and creamy white of the first version with a dark, almost blackish gray and a warm taupe. This bolder palette creates more contrast within the striped section of the quilt. As the three fabrics in this version are more balanced in terms of their intensity, the squares at the top of the composition are not as graphically bold as those in the first version.

FINISHED QUILT SIZE
54½" x 70½" (140 cm x 180.5 cm)

FABRICS
The fabric amounts are based on using 44–45" (112–115 cm) wide fabrics.

COLORWAY 1
OFF-WHITE, GRAY, AND RED

FABRIC 1: 1⅔ yards (1.5 m) of a solid oyster, such as Robert Kaufman *Kona Cotton Solids* in Oyster (1268)

FABRIC 2: 2 yards (1.9 m) of a solid light gray, such as Robert Kaufman *Kona Cotton Solids* in Ash (1007)

FABRIC 3: ¼ yard (25 cm) of a solid red, such as Robert Kaufman *Kona Cotton Solids* in Coral (1087)

BACKING FABRIC: 3½ yards (3.2 m) of desired fabric

BINDING FABRIC: ½ yard (50 cm) more of Fabric 2

COLORWAY 2
OFF-WHITE, BLACK, AND RED

FABRIC 1: 1⅔ yards (1.5 m) of a solid off-white, such as FreeSpirit *Designer Solids* in Natural (S44)

FABRIC 2: 2 yards (1.9 m) of a solid black, such as Robert Kaufman *Kona Cotton Solids* in Pepper (359)

FABRIC 3: ¼ yard (25 cm) of a red, white, gray, and black small-scale print, such as DS Quilts Collection *Richmond Small Geo* in Red

BACKING FABRIC: 3½ yards (3.2 m) of desired fabric

BINDING FABRIC: ½ yard (50 cm) more of Fabric 1

OTHER MATERIALS
+ 59" x 75" (150 cm x 191 cm) piece of batting (or a twin-sized package)

+ All-purpose thread for piecing

+ Off-white quilting thread for both colorways

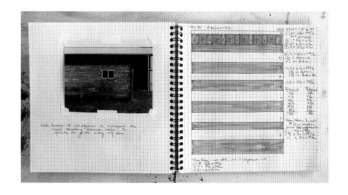

CUT THE QUILT-TOP PIECES

1. Using a rotary cutter, straight edge, and a cutting mat, cut a 54½" (139 cm) x width of fabric (WOF) piece of Fabric 1, cutting from selvage to selvage. Subcut this piece *lengthwise* into one 2½" x 54½" (6.5 cm x 139 cm) strip for one A piece; one 4½" x 54½" (11.5 cm x 139 cm) strip for one F piece; and four 6½" x 54½" (16.5 cm x 139 cm) strips for four D pieces. Pin a label to your pieces as you cut them.

2. From Fabric 2, cut a 54½" (139 cm) x WOF piece of fabric. Subcut this piece *lengthwise* into two 4½" x 54½" (11.5 cm x 139 cm) strips for two C pieces, one 8½" x 54½" (22 cm x 139 cm) strip for one G piece, and four 6½" x 54½" strips. Keep three of the 6½" x 54½" strips for three E pieces. Subcut the last 6½" x 54½" (16.5 cm x 139 cm) strip into two 4½" x 6½" (11.5 cm x 16.5 cm) rectangles for two H pieces, and five 2½" x 6½" (6.5 cm x 16.5 cm) strips for five K pieces.

3. From Fabric 3, cut a 6½" (16.5 cm) x WOF strip of fabric. Subcut this strip into six 6½" x 6½" (16.5 cm x 16.5 cm) squares for six J pieces.

CONSTRUCT THE QUILT TOP

4. Following the diagram, construct the pieced row B. With right sides together and using a ¼" (6 mm) seam allowance for all seams, sew one H piece to one J square, then sew one K piece to the other side of this J square. Continue in this way, sewing on a J square and a K piece alternately until you have one J square remaining. Sew on the remaining J square, followed by the remaining H piece. Press all seams to the side.

5. Following the quilt layout diagram, sew the A strip to the top of the pieced Row B, then sew one C strip to the bottom of row B. Continue adding on strips from top to bottom in this way, next adding on one D strip, followed by one E strip, the F strip, another E strip, another D strip, the last E strip, another D strip, the last C strip, the last D strip, and lastly the G strip to complete the quilt top. Press all seams to the side.

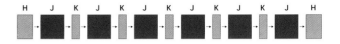

4   *Sewing together the pieces for row B.*

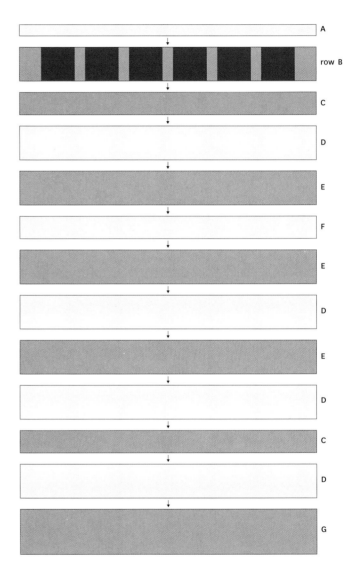

5   *Sewing the strips together to complete the quilt top.*

CUT AND PIECE THE QUILT BACK

6   To make the quilt back, cut two 62" (157.5 cm) x WOF pieces out of the backing fabric. Trimming off the selvages as you do so, trim each of the strips *lengthwise* so that they measure 39½" x 62" (100.5 cm x 157.5 cm). Sew the pieces right sides together, along one long edge, and press the seam allowances to the side.

FINISH THE QUILT

7   Layer the quilt top, batting, and quilt back to make a quilt sandwich (page 29). Baste together with quilting pins or basting stitches (page 30).

8   Quilt as desired (page 31). After quilting, trim off the excess batting and backing fabric to align them with the edges of the quilt top, and square up all sides of the quilt if necessary.

9   From the binding fabric, cut seven 2½" (6 cm) x WOF strips. Cut off the selvages and sew the seven strips together end-to-end to create the continuous binding strip (page 31). Bind the quilt as desired (page 33).

franklin No. 1

The inspiration for this design was a Churn Dash quilt made by my maternal great-great aunt, Ollie Langsdon. Aunt Ollie lived with my grandparents for a while so I was lucky enough to know her, at least for a few years when I was a young child. She was the only person in my family who quilted. My mom and I still have a few of her quilts, including the one that I based Franklin on, probably made sometime in the 1960s or 1970s. The pattern of the original quilt is called Churn Dash. It is a very traditional quilt block that dates to the 1800s and was inspired by the design of a butter churn. My favorite part of the quilt is the one "mistake" block that Aunt Ollie included in the last row at the bottom, where she flipped one of the half-square triangles upside down. My assumption is that she did this on purpose, as it was common practice back then for quilt makers to include a "humility" block in their works.

In the first version of the quilt, I've used forty different vintage-inspired cotton prints, so each block is different, paired with a neutral solid cream background color. Notice how the points on the Churn Dash shapes make them dance and spin across the surface—a movement intensified by the striped prints. I intentionally chose fabrics similar in feel to my Aunt Ollie's so that the two quilts look like they could have been made around the same time.

My second version is made in a slightly different way, so it has its own set of instructions starting on page 70.

FINISHED QUILT SIZE

60½" x 75½" (153 cm x 191 cm)

FABRICS

The fabric amounts are based on using 44-45" (112-115 cm) wide fabrics.

FABRIC 1: 4 yards (3.7 m) of a solid off-white, such as FreeSpirit *Designer Solids* in Natural (S44)

FABRIC 2: ⅛ yard—or a 10" (25 cm) square—of each of 40 different printed cotton fabrics

BACKING FABRIC: 4 yards (3.7 m) more of Fabric 1

BINDING FABRIC: ½ yard (50 cm) more of Fabric 1

OTHER MATERIALS

+ 65" x 80" (163 cm x 201 cm) piece of batting (or a twin-sized package)

+ All-purpose thread for piecing

+ Off-white quilting thread

CUT THE QUILT-TOP PIECES

1 Using a rotary cutter, straight edge, and a cutting mat, cut ten 8" (20.2 cm) x width of fabric (WOF) strips from Fabric 1, cutting from selvage to selvage. Subcut each of these strips into four 8" x 8" (20.2 cm x 20.2 cm) squares for 40 A pieces. Pin a label to your pieces as you cut them.

2 From Fabric 1, cut eight 4" (10.1 cm) x WOF strips. Subcut each of these strips into ten 4" x 4" (10.1 cm x 10.1 cm) squares for a total of 80 B squares, to be used when constructing the B/C half-square-triangle squares for the Churn Dash blocks.

3 From Fabric 1, cut eight 2" (5 cm) x WOF strips. Subcut each of these strips into twenty 2" x 2" (5 cm x 5 cm) squares, for a total of 160 D pieces.

4 From Fabric 1, cut two 2" (5 cm) x WOF strips. Subcut each of these strips into twenty 2" x 2" (5 cm x 5 cm) squares for 40 F pieces.

5 From each of the 40 printed fabrics (Fabric 2), cut two 4" x 4" (10.1 cm x 10.1 cm) for a total of 80 C squares, to be used when constructing the B/C half-square-triangle squares for the Churn Dash blocks. Pin together each pair cut from the same fabric because each pair will be used in its own Churn Dash block.

6 From each of the 40 printed fabrics (Fabric 2), cut four 2" x 2" (5 cm x 5 cm) squares, for a total of 160 E pieces. Pin each set of four E squares cut from the same fabric to the C squares cut from the same fabric to keep the matching sets together.

CONSTRUCT THE PIECED D/E RECTANGLES

7 Take a 2" x 2" (5 cm x 5 cm) E square from one of the sets of four E squares cut from the same fabric (cut in step 6). Stitch this E square to a 2" x 2" (5 cm x 5 cm) D square in Fabric 1 (cut in step 3), with right sides together and using a ¼" (6 mm) seam allowance for all seams. Open out this pieced rectangle and press the seam toward the printed fabric. Make three more pieced rectangles in this way using the three remaining E squares cut from the same fabric and three more D squares in Fabric 1. These four matching 2" x 3½" (5 cm x 8.8 cm) D/E pieced rectangles will be used in one Churn Dash block. Keep them together with their matching printed C squares.

8 Repeat step 7 for each of the remaining 39 sets of four E squares. You now have the four D/E rectangles you will need for each of the 40 Churn Dash blocks.

CONSTRUCT THE B/C HALF-SQUARE-TRIANGLE SQUARES

9 Using the 80 B squares in Fabric 1 and the 80 C squares in Fabric 2 (the printed fabrics), make 160 B/C half-square-triangle squares following steps 10–13 for the Franklin No. 2 quilt (page 72). (Be careful to keep each set of four matching B/C squares together with their other matching pieces.)

CONSTRUCT THE CHURN DASH BLOCKS

10 To make the first block, take a matching set of four B/C squares and four D/E rectangles. To begin, sew together the first row at the top of the block. Following the diagram, sew one B/C square to one D/E rectangle, with right sides together and using a ¼" (6 mm) seam allowance for all seams. Sew another B/C square to the opposite side of the D/E rectangle to complete the top row of the block. Press the seams toward the center.

11 Following the diagram, sew one D/E rectangle to one F square in Fabric 1 (cut in step 4). Sew another D/E rectangle to the opposite side of the F square to complete the middle row of the block. Press the seams toward the D/E rectangles.

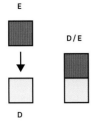

E

D/E

D

7   *Making the D/E rectangles.*

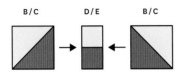

B/C   D/E   B/C

10   *Sewing together the top row of the Churn Dash block.*

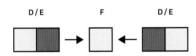

D/E   F   D/E

11   *Sewing together the middle row of the Churn Dash block.*

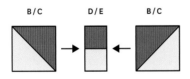

B/C   D/E   B/C

12   *Sewing together the bottom row of the Churn Dash block.*

12 Following the diagram, sew one B/C square to one D/E rectangle. Sew another B/C square to the opposite side of the D/E rectangle to complete the bottom row of the block. Press the seams toward the center.

13 Sew the top row to the middle row, nesting the seams between rows. Sew the bottom row to the other side of the middle row, nesting the seams, to complete the block.

14 Repeat steps 10–13 to make 38 more blocks, using matching sets of four B/C squares and four D/E rectangles, and one F square in Fabric 1, for each block—to make a total of 39 Churn Dash blocks.

15 For the last block, repeat steps 10–13, but change the orientation of triangles in the last B/C square in the bottom row, following the diagram.

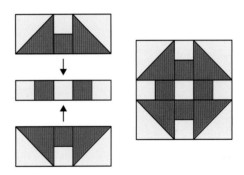

13   *Completing the Churn Dash block.*

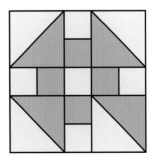

15   *Making one "mistake" block.*

CONSTRUCT THE QUILT TOP

16 Select five Churn Dash blocks for row 1 at the top of the quilt. Following the diagram, sew together these five Churn Dash blocks and three A squares in the sequence shown, to construct row 1 (the top row of the quilt). Press all seams toward the right. Repeat to make a total of five rows in the same way.

17 Select three Churn Dash blocks for row 2 of the quilt top. Following the diagram, sew together these three Churn Dash blocks and five A squares in the sequence shown, to construct row 2 of the quilt top. Press all seams toward the left. Repeat to make a total of five rows in the same way.

18 Sew row 1 to row 2. Then following the diagram, continue to sew the rows together, alternating the rows with five Churn Dash blocks with those with three Churn Dash blocks as shown, until all the rows are joined together, making sure to keep the row with the mistake block last. Press all seams to the side.

CUT AND PIECE THE QUILT BACK

19 To make the quilt back, cut two 68" (173 cm) x WOF pieces out of the backing fabric. Trimming off the selvages as you do so, trim each of the pieces *lengthwise* so that they measure 41½" x 68" (105.5 cm x 173 cm). Sew the pieces right sides together, along one long edge, and press the seam allowances to the side.

FINISH THE QUILT

20 Layer the quilt top, batting, and quilt back to make a quilt sandwich (page 29). Baste together with quilting pins or basting stitches (page 30).

21 Quilt as desired (page 31). After quilting, trim off the excess batting and backing fabric to align them with the edges of the quilt top, and square up all sides of the quilt if necessary.

22 From the binding fabric, cut seven 2½" (6 cm) x WOF strips. Cut off the selvages and sew the seven strips together end-to-end to create the continuous binding (page 31). Bind the quilt as desired (page 33).

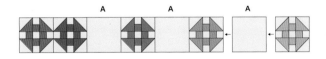

16 *Sewing together row 1 of the quilt top.*

17 *Sewing together row 2 of the quilt top.*

18 *Sewing together the quilt top rows.*

franklin No. 2

Like Franklin No. 1 on page 64, this quilt is a contemporary take on the traditional design. It is made with two yarn-dyed linen/cotton blend fabrics, so all forty of the Churn Dash blocks, with the exception of the "humility" one, are identical. With its rough texture and coarse weave, the fabric has a vintage feel. However, I think this version looks more modern than Franklin No. 1, as the two fabrics read more as solids, albeit with a beautiful variation of color within each one.

The gray-blue fabric is cooler in temperature than the warmer beige that I paired it with, which makes the negative space (background) recede. The subtle play of the warm beige against the gray-blue creates a more reserved color palette than that of the first, more traditional version on page 64. But if you contemplate the composition for a while you can see that despite the more subtle color scheme, the Churn Dash shapes still pop and twist against the darker ground.

FINISHED QUILT SIZE

60½" x 75½" (153 cm x 191 cm)

FABRICS

The fabric amounts are based on using 44–45" (112–115 cm) wide fabrics.

FABRIC 1: 4 yards (3.7 m) of a solid light gray-blue, such as Robert Kaufman *Essex Yarn Dyed* linen/cotton blend in Indigo (1178)

FABRIC 2: 1½ yards (1.4 m) of a solid light beige, such as Robert Kaufman *Essex Yarn Dyed* linen/cotton blend in Flax (1143)

BACKING FABRIC: 4 yards (3.7 m) more of Fabric 1

BINDING FABRIC: ½ yard (50 cm) more of Fabric 1

OTHER MATERIALS

+ 65" x 80" (163 cm x 201 cm) piece of batting (or a twin-sized package)

+ All-purpose thread for piecing

+ Off-white quilting thread

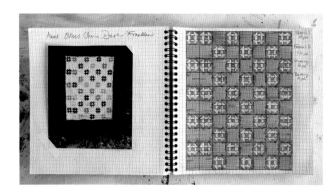

CUT THE QUILT-TOP PIECES

1. Using a rotary cutter, straight edge, and a cutting mat, cut ten 8" (20.2 cm) x width of fabric (WOF) strips from Fabric 1, cutting from selvage to selvage. Subcut each of these strips into four 8" x 8" (20.2 cm x 20.2 cm) squares for 40 A pieces. Pin a label to your pieces as you cut them.

2. From Fabric 1, cut eight 4" (10.1 cm) x WOF strips. Subcut each of these strips into ten 4" x 4" (10.1 cm x 10.1 cm) squares, for a total of 80 B squares, to be used when constructing the B/C half-square-triangle squares.

3. From Fabric 1, cut eight 2" (5 cm) x WOF strips, to be used for the D pieces when constructing the pieced D/E rectangles.

4. From Fabric 1, cut two 2" (5 cm) x WOF strips. Subcut each of these strips into twenty 2" x 2" (5 cm x 5 cm) squares for 40 F pieces.

5. From Fabric 2, cut eight 4" (10.1 cm) x WOF strips. Subcut each of these strips into ten 4" x 4" (10.1 cm x 10.1 cm) squares, for a total of 80 C squares, to be used when constructing the B/C half-square-triangle squares for the Churn Dash blocks.

6. From Fabric 2, cut eight 2" (5 cm) x WOF strips, to be used for the E pieces when constructing the pieced D/E rectangles.

CONSTRUCT THE D/E RECTANGLES

7. Using the 2" (5 cm) x WOF strips of Fabric 1 and Fabric 2 (cut in steps 3 and 6), place one Fabric 1 strip on top of one Fabric 2 strip, with right sides together, and sew them together along one long edge of the strips, using a ¼" (6 mm) seam allowance. Open out the joined strip and press the seam allowances to the side, toward the darker fabric.

8. Repeat step 7 seven more times with the remaining 2" (5 cm) strips of Fabric 1 and Fabric 2.

9. Cut each of the eight pieced strips into twenty 2" x 3½" (5 cm x 8.8 cm) pieces for 160 pieced D/E rectangles.

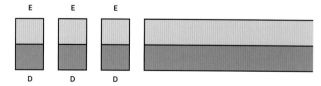

9 *Cutting the D/E rectangles from the pieced strips.*

CONSTRUCT THE B/C HALF-SQUARE-TRIANGLE SQUARES

10. Using a pencil and a straight edge, draw a line diagonally across the center of each of the 4" x 4" (10.1 cm x 10.1 cm) B squares (Fabric 1) on the wrong side of the fabric. Then, measure ¼" (6 mm) from the center line and draw a line on each side of the center line, for a total of three lines on the wrong side of the fabric. Repeat this step for all 80 B squares.

11. Place one B square on top of one C square (Fabric 2), with right sides together and the drawn lines facing up, and pin in place. Stitch along the two outer drawn lines on the square.

12. After the two lines have been stitched, cut the square apart down the center line. Open out each pieced square and press seam allowances to the side, toward the darker fabric. These B/C squares each measure 3½" x 3½" (8.8 cm x 8.8 cm).

13. Repeat steps 11 and 12 with the remaining 79 B and 79 C squares to make a total of 160 B/C half-square-triangle squares.

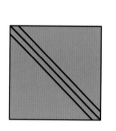

10 *Drawing diagonal lines on the wrong side of the B squares.*

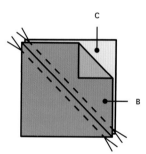

11 *Sewing the B and C squares together.*

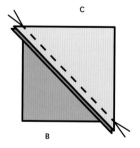
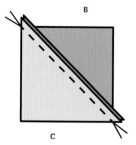

12 *Cutting the joined squares in half diagonally to form two half-square-triangle squares.*

CONSTRUCT THE CHURN DASH BLOCKS

14 Following the diagram, sew one B/C square to one D/E rectangle, with right sides together and using a ¼" (6 mm) seam allowance for all seams. Sew another B/C square to the opposite side of the D/E rectangle to complete the top row of the block. Press the seams toward the center.

15 Following the diagram, sew one D/E rectangle to one F square. Sew another D/E rectangle to the opposite side of the F square to complete the middle row of the block. Press the seams toward the D/E rectangles.

16 Following the diagram, sew one B/C square to one D/E rectangle. Sew another B/C square to the opposite side of the D/E rectangle to complete the bottom row of the block. Press the seams toward the center.

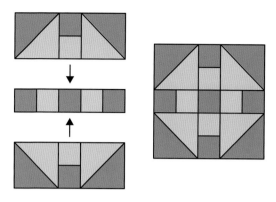

17 *Completing the Churn Dash block.*

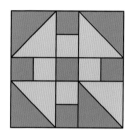

19 *Making one "mistake" block.*

17 Sew the top row to the middle row, nesting the seams between rows. Sew the bottom row to the other side of the middle row, nesting the seams, to complete the block.

18 Repeat steps 14–17 to make 38 more blocks, using four B/C squares, four D/E rectangles, and one F square for each block—to make a total of 39 Churn Dash blocks.

19 For the last block, repeat steps 14–17, but change the orientation of triangles in the last B/C square in the bottom row, following the diagram.

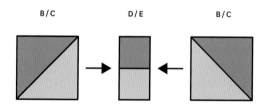

B/C   D/E   B/C

14 *Sewing together the top row of the Churn Dash block.*

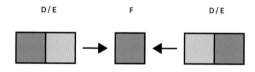

D/E   F   D/E

15 *Sewing together the middle row of the Churn Dash block.*

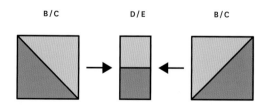

B/C   D/E   B/C

16 *Sewing together the bottom row of the Churn Dash block.*

CONSTRUCT THE QUILT TOP

20 Following the diagram, sew together five Churn Dash blocks and three A squares in the sequence shown, to construct row 1 (the top row of the quilt). Press all seams toward the right. Repeat to make a total of five rows in the same way.

21 Following the diagram, sew together three Churn Dash blocks and five A squares in the sequence shown, to construct row 2 of the quilt top. Press all seams toward the left. Repeat to make a total of five rows in the same way.

22 Sew row 1 to row 2. Then following the diagram, continue to sew the rows together, alternating the rows with five Churn Dash blocks with those with three Churn Dash blocks as shown, until all the rows are joined together, making sure to keep the row with the mistake block last. Press all seams to the side.

CUT AND PIECE THE QUILT BACK

23 To make the quilt back, cut two 68" (173 cm) x WOF pieces out of the backing fabric. Trimming off the selvages as you do so, trim each of the pieces *lengthwise* so that they measure 41½" x 68" (105.5 cm x 173 cm). Sew the pieces right sides together, along one long edge, and press the seam allowances to the side.

FINISH THE QUILT

24 Layer the quilt top, batting, and quilt back to make a quilt sandwich (page 29). Baste together with quilting pins or basting stitches (page 30).

25 Quilt as desired (page 31). After quilting, trim off the excess batting and backing fabric to align them with the edges of the quilt top, and square up all sides of the quilt if necessary.

26 From the binding fabric, cut seven 2½" (6 cm) x WOF strips. Cut off the selvages and sew the seven strips together end-to-end to create the continuous binding (page 31). Bind the quilt as desired (page 33).

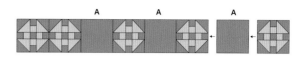

20 *Sewing together row 1 of the quilt top.*

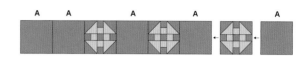

21 *Sewing together row 2 of the quilt top.*

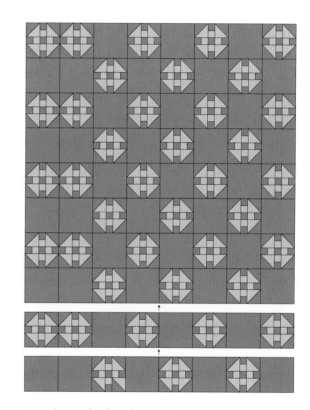

22 *Sewing together the quilt-top rows.*

dayton No. 1

This quilt was inspired by a church in Dayton, Ohio. I came across the building while I was visiting a salvage store across the street and was immediately drawn to the stone cross inlaid in the surface of one of the exterior walls. I thought the contrast in both color and texture of the two materials was especially beautiful. For my quilt design based on these elements, I focused only on one section of the wall and experimented with the amount of negative space combined with the simple cross shape. In the final version of the pattern, I constructed a patchwork cross block and placed it in the lower left-hand side of the quilt.

Two colors that were similar to the actual colors of the brick wall and cross, but not an exact duplication of them, feature in the first version of the quilt. The colors that I chose—a bright orange cotton chambray paired with a yellowish cream chambray—are much more intense and saturated than the colors of the brick and stonework of the church. The orange fabric is a highly saturated and high-value color, and when combined with the yellowish cream fabric, it forms an analogous color scheme, because orange and yellow sit next to each other on the color wheel. This version of the quilt feels almost like a wholecloth quilt with a single patchwork block, due to the fact that there is such a large amount of orange fabric in the background and only a small amount of cream in the patchwork cross. (See page 84 for the other version of Dayton.)

FINISHED QUILT SIZE

Finished 58½" x 70½"
(148 cm x 178 cm)

FABRICS

The fabric amounts are based on using 44–45" (112–115 cm) wide fabrics.

FABRIC 1: 3½ yards (3.2 m) of a solid tangerine orange, such as Robert Kaufman *Kona Cotton Solids* in Tangerine (1370)

FABRIC 2: ¼ yard (25 cm) of a solid pale yellow, such as Robert Kaufman *Interweave Chambray* in Buttercup (136)

BACKING FABRIC: 4 yards (3.7 m) of a solid light denim blue, such as Robert Kaufman *Interweave Chambray* in Denim (67)

BINDING FABRIC: ½ yard (50 cm) more of Fabric 1

OTHER MATERIALS

+ 63" x 75" (157 cm x 187 cm) piece of batting (or a twin-sized package)

+ All-purpose thread for piecing

+ Cream quilting thread

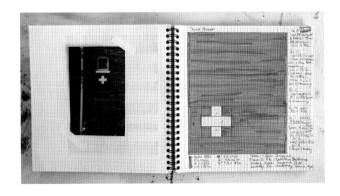

CUT THE QUILT-TOP PIECES

1   Using a rotary cutter, straight edge, and a cutting mat, cut one 58½" (148.2 cm) x width of fabric (WOF) piece from Fabric 1, cutting from selvage to selvage. Trim off the selvages and trim the strip *lengthwise* so that it measures 42½" x 58½" (107.7 cm x 148.2 cm) for one A piece. Pin a label to your pieces as you cut them.

2   From Fabric 1, cut one 58½" (148.2 cm) x WOF piece. Subcut this piece *lengthwise* into one 10½" x 58½" (26.7 cm x 148.2 cm) strip for one D piece and one 18½" x 58½" (46.2 cm x 148.2 cm) strip. Trim the 18½" x 58½" (46.2 cm x 148.2 cm) strip so that it measures 18½" x 32½" (46.2 cm x 82.7 cm) for one C piece.

3   From the remaining Fabric 1 left over from step 2, cut one 8½" x 18½" (21.7 cm x 46.2 cm) rectangle for one B piece and four 6½" x 6½" (16.2 cm x 16.2 cm) squares for four E pieces.

4   From Fabric 2, cut one 6½" (16.2 cm) x WOF strip. Subcut this strip into two 6½" x 6½" (16.2 cm x 16.2 cm) squares for two F pieces and one 6½" x 18½" (16.2 cm x 46.2 cm) rectangle for one G piece.

CONSTRUCT THE QUILT TOP

5   Following the diagram, sew one E piece to one F piece, with right sides together and using a ¼" (6 mm) seam allowance for all seams. Sew another E piece to the opposite side of the F piece. Sew the remaining two E pieces to the remaining F piece in the same way. Press the seams to the side, toward the darker fabric.

6   Sew one of the pieced sections made in step 5 to the top of the G piece. Sew the other pieced section made in step 5 to the bottom of the G piece to complete the cross block. Press the seams to the side, toward the darker fabric.

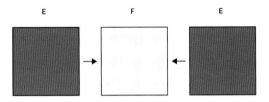

E   F   E

5   *Sewing together the top and bottom of the cross block.*

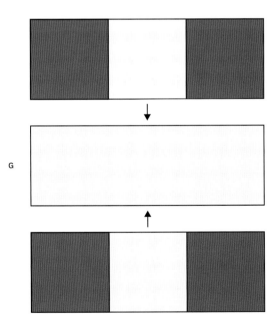

G

6   *Completing the cross block.*

7 Following the diagram, sew the B piece to one side of the cross block and the C piece to the other side. Press the seams away from the cross block.

8 Sew the A piece to the top of the pieced section and press the seam allowances toward the A piece. Sew the D piece to the bottom of the pieced section and press the seam allowances toward the D piece.

CUT AND PIECE THE QUILT BACK

9 To make the quilt back, cut two 66" (168 cm) x WOF pieces out of the backing fabric. Trimming off the selvages as you do so, trim each of the strips *lengthwise* so that they measure 39½" x 66" (100.5 cm x 168 cm). Sew the pieces right sides together, along one long edge, and press the seam allowances to the side.

FINISH THE QUILT

10 Layer the quilt top, batting, and quilt back to make a quilt sandwich (page 29). Baste together with quilting pins or basting stitches (page 30).

11 Quilt as desired (page 31). After quilting, trim off the excess batting and backing fabric to align them with the edges of the quilt top, and square up all sides of the quilt if necessary.

12 From the binding fabric, cut seven 2½" (6 cm) x WOF strips. Cut off the selvages and sew the seven strips together end-to-end to create the continuous binding strip (page 31). Bind the quilt as desired (page 33).

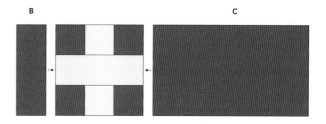

7 Sewing the side pieces to the cross block.

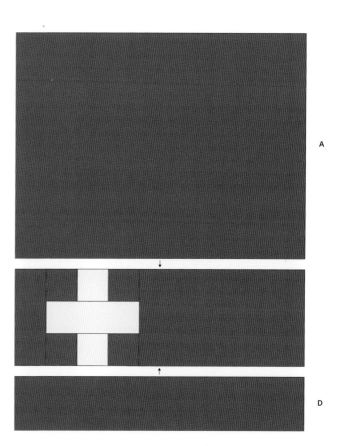

8 Sewing on the top and bottom pieces of the quilt.

dayton No. 2

Like Dayton No. 1, this quilt was inspired by the exterior brick wall of a church with a stone cross inlaid in it. For the second version of the quilt, I used three colors instead of just two, although the two colors of the first version feature in this color palette as well. I changed the background of the design to an oregano-colored green, which is much more muted and less intense than the orange in the first version.

In the area around the cross block I created a band of color to break up the negative space, and for this I chose the yellowish cream chambray used for the cross in the first version. The intense orange features only sparingly in this patchwork cross, making it less visually jarring than it is in the first version. The intensity of the orange is also softened by the two less-saturated colors—cream and muted green—surrounding it. The band of cream and the addition of a third color gives the overall composition more movement than the first version of the quilt.

FINISHED QUILT SIZE

Finished 58½" x 70½" (148 cm x 178 cm)

FABRICS

The fabric amounts are based on using 44–45" (112–115 cm) wide fabrics.

FABRIC 1: 3½ yards (3.2 m) of a solid dusty green, such as Robert Kaufman *Interweave Chambray* in Oregano (273)

FABRIC 2: ¾ yard (70 cm) of a solid pale yellow, such as Robert Kaufman *Interweave Chambray* in Buttercup (136)

FABRIC 3: ¼ yard (25 cm) of a solid tangerine orange, such as Robert Kaufman *Kona Cotton Solids* in Tangerine (1370)

BACKING FABRIC: 4 yards (3.7 m) of a solid light denim blue, such as Robert Kaufman *Interweave Chambray* in Denim (67)

BINDING FABRIC: ½ yard (50 cm) more of Fabric 1

OTHER MATERIALS

+ 63" x 75" (157 cm x 187 cm) piece of batting (or a twin-sized package)

+ All-purpose thread for piecing

+ Cream quilting thread

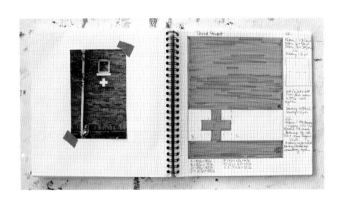

CUT THE QUILT-TOP PIECES

1 Using a rotary cutter, straight edge, and a cutting mat, cut one 58½" (148.2 cm) x width of fabric (WOF) piece from Fabric 1, cutting from selvage to selvage. Trim off the selvages and trim the strip *lengthwise* so that it measures 42½" x 58½" (107.7 cm x 148.2 cm) for one A piece. Pin a label to your pieces as you cut them.

2 From Fabric 1, cut one 58½" (148.2 cm) x WOF piece. Subcut this piece *lengthwise* into one 10½" x 58½" (26.7 cm x 148.2 cm) strip for one D piece.

3 From Fabric 2, cut one 18½" (46.2 cm) x WOF strip. Subcut this strip into one 8½" x 18½" (21.7 cm x 46.2 cm) rectangle for one B piece and one 18½" x 32½" (46.2 cm x 82.7 cm) rectangle for one C piece.

4 From Fabric 2, cut one 6½" (16.2 cm) x WOF strip. Subcut this strip into four 6½" x 6½" (16.2 cm x 16.2 cm) squares for four E pieces.

5 From Fabric 3, cut one 6½" (16.2 cm) x WOF strip. Subcut this strip into two 6½" x 6½" (16.2 cm x 16.2 cm) squares for two F pieces and one 6½" x 18½" (16.2 cm x 46.2 cm) rectangle for one G piece.

CONSTRUCT THE QUILT TOP

6 Following the diagram, sew one E piece to one F piece, with right sides together and using a ¼" (6 mm) seam allowance for all seams. Sew another E piece to the opposite side of the F piece. Sew the remaining two E pieces to the remaining F piece in the same way. Press the seams to the side, toward the darker fabric.

7 Sew one of the pieced sections made in step 6 to the top of the G piece. Sew the other pieced section made in step 5 to the bottom of the G piece to complete the cross block. Press the seams to the side, toward the darker fabric.

8 Following the diagram, sew the B piece to one side of the the cross block and the C piece to the other side. Press the seams away from the cross block.

9 Sew the A piece to the top of the pieced section and press the seam allowances toward the A piece. Sew the D piece to the bottom of the pieced section and press the seam allowances toward the D piece.

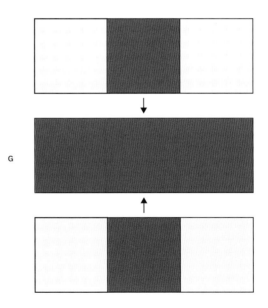

E F E

6 *Sewing together the top and bottom of the cross block.*

7 *Completing the cross block.*

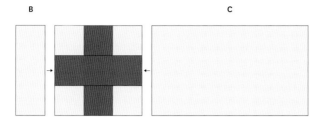

B   C

8   *Sewing the side pieces to the cross block.*

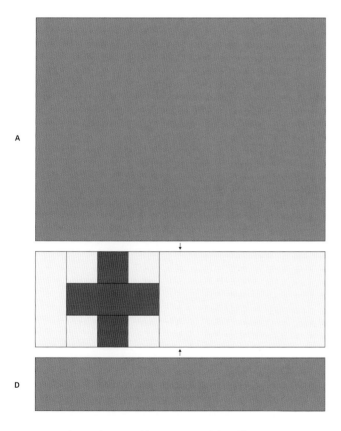

A

D

9   *Sewing on the top and bottom pieces of the quilt.*

CUT AND PIECE THE QUILT BACK

10   To make the quilt back, cut two 66" (168 cm) x WOF pieces out of the backing fabric. Trimming off the selvages as you do so, trim each of the strips *lengthwise* so that they measure 39½" x 66" (100.5 cm x 168 cm). Sew the pieces right sides together, along one long edge, and press the seam allowances to the side.

FINISH THE QUILT

11   Layer the quilt top, batting, and quilt back to make a quilt sandwich (page 29). Baste together with quilting pins or basting stitches (page 30).

12   Quilt as desired (page 31). After quilting, trim off the excess batting and backing fabric to align them with the edges of the quilt top, and square up all sides of the quilt if necessary.

13   From the binding fabric, cut seven 2½" (6 cm) x WOF strips. Cut off the selvages and sew the seven strips together end-to-end to create the continuous binding strip (page 31). Bind the quilt as desired (page 33).

shellshock

Most of the quilts in this book were inspired by a place—this is one of the few exceptions. It was inspired by one of my favorite paintings by my husband, Jeffrey Cortland Jones, called *Shellshock*; it was included in the *New American Paintings* art periodical in the summer of 2013. Fine art is truly part of my environment and everyday life because my husband is a painter and a professor of art at the University of Dayton, and his work is exhibited in galleries and exhibitions throughout the United States. Most of his paintings are very minimal and abstract, and made with thin layers of enamel paint. I love the area of intense yellow surrounded by more subtle, neutral shades of white and cream in *Shellshock*, and that is what I concentrated on when designing this quilt.

In the first version of the quilt I took my color palette directly from the painting. I used a creamy warm yellowish cream for the background, or negative space, and I combined it with a bright white and two solid yellows, a bright lemon hue and a darker saffron. The overall palette includes both warm and cool temperatures, as the background color and the two yellows are warm, while the white is cool. Because the colors are more intense in the patchwork section in the center of the quilt, the eye is drawn to that area of the design. The background of the composition is much less intense in saturation, which provides a place for the eye to rest and makes the center portion appear to float.

I created my own color scheme for the second version of this quilt. The overall temperature of the palette is cooler than that of the first version. The background is a neutral beige-colored cotton. For the center section I selected a bone white that is less saturated than the background, a saturated solid lime cotton, and a more muted solid dark blue cotton. In the first version of the quilt the eye is drawn to the saffron in the pieced section in the middle, but in this one it is drawn to the blue, because it is placed next to the intense saturated green, and they bounce off of each other. I love the combination of muted neutral colors combined with more highly saturated hues in this version. Because the saturated fabrics are used somewhat sparingly, and don't make up the entire quilt top, the composition has a calm flow.

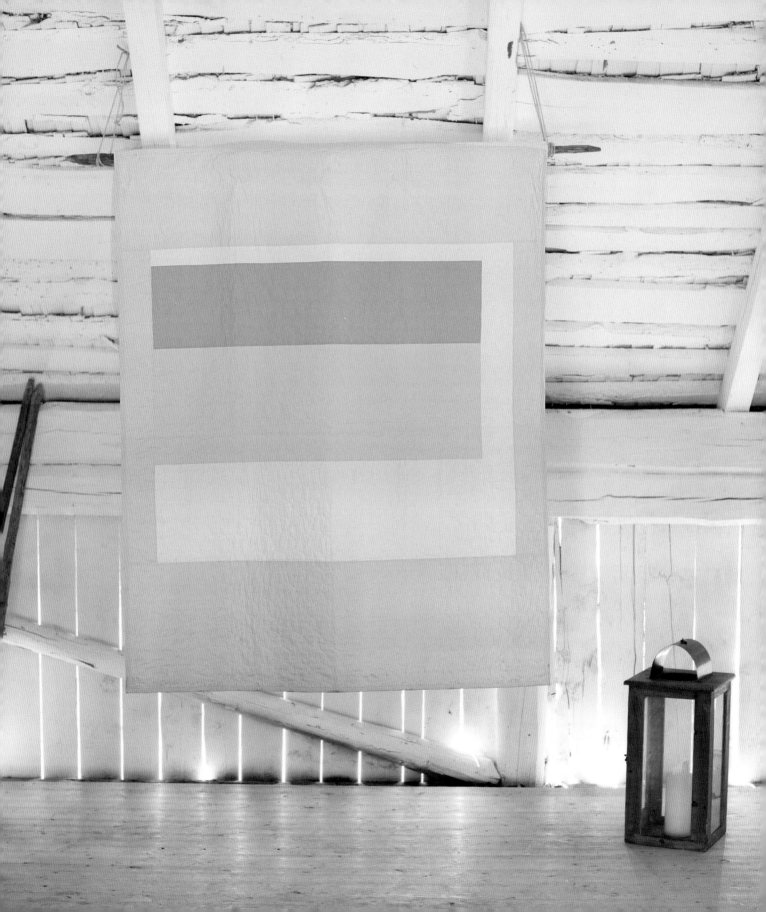

54½" x 66½" (138 cm x 169 cm)

FABRICS

The fabric amounts are based on using 44–45" (112–115 cm) wide fabrics.

COLORWAY 1
CREAM, WHITE, AND YELLOWS

FABRIC 1: 1¾ yards (1.6 m) of a solid cream, such as FreeSpirit *Designer Solids* in Chamois (S45)

FABRIC 2: 1¼ yards (1.2 m) of a solid white, such as FreeSpirit *Designer Solids* in Winter White (S29)

FABRIC 3: 1¼ yards (1.2 m) of a solid saffron yellow, such as *Designer Solids* in Saffron (S46)

FABRIC 4: 1¼ yards (1.2 m) of a solid light yellow, such as FreeSpirit *Designer Solids* in Lemon (S26)

BACKING FABRIC: 3½ yards (3.2 m) more of Fabric 4

BINDING FABRIC: ½ yard (50 cm) more of Fabric 1

COLORWAY 2
GRAY, WHITE, GREEN, AND NAVY

FABRIC 1: 2 yards (1.9 m) of a solid taupe, such as FreeSpirit *Designer Solids* in Dogwood (S35)

FABRIC 2: 1¼ yards (1.2 m) of a solid off-white, such as FreeSpirit *Designer Solids* in Natural (S44)

FABRIC 3: 1¼ yards (1.2 m) of a solid light lime green, such as Robert Kaufman *Kona Cotton Solids* in Chartreuse (1072)

FABRIC 4: 1¼ yards (1.2 m) of a solid navy, such as FreeSpirit *Designer Solids* in Cosmic Blue (S76)

BACKING FABRIC: 3½ yards (3.2 m) more of Fabric 1

BINDING FABRIC: ½ yard (50 cm) more of Fabric 1

OTHER MATERIALS

+ 59" x 71" (148 cm x 179 cm) piece of batting (or a twin-sized package)

+ All-purpose thread for piecing

+ White quilting thread for colorway 1, OR off-white for colorway 2

CUT THE QUILT-TOP PIECES

1   Using a rotary cutter, straight edge, and a cutting mat, cut one 54½" (138.2 cm) x width of fabric (WOF) piece from Fabric 1, cutting from selvage to selvage. Subcut this piece *lengthwise* into one 12½" x 54½" (31.7 cm x 138.2 cm) strip for one A piece, one 16½" x 54½" (41.7 cm x 138.2 cm) strip for one H piece, and two 4½" x 54½" (11.2 x 138.2 cm) strips. Trim each of the two 4½" x 54½" (11.2 x 138.2 cm) strips so that they measure 4½" x 38½" (11.2 x 97.7 cm) for two B pieces. Pin a label to your pieces as you cut them.

2   From Fabric 2, cut one 42½" (108.2 cm) x WOF piece. Subcut this piece *lengthwise* into one 2½" x 42½" (6.2 cm x 108.2 cm) strip for one C piece, one 12½" x 42½" (31.7 cm x 108.2 cm) strip for one F piece, and one 4½" x 42½" (11.2 x 108.2 cm) strip. Trim the 4½" x 42½" (11.2 x 108.2 cm) strip so that it measures 4½" x 38½" (11.2 x 97.7 cm) for one G piece.

3   From Fabric 3, cut one 42½" (108.2 cm) x WOF piece. Subcut this piece *lengthwise* into one 10½" x 42½" (26.7 cm x 108.2 cm) strip for one D piece.

4   From Fabric 4, cut one 42½" (108.2 cm) x WOF piece. Subcut this piece *lengthwise* into one 14½" x 42½" (36.7 cm x 108.2 cm) strip for one E piece.

CONSTRUCT THE QUILT TOP

5   Following the diagram, sew together the four horizontal strips at the center of the quilt. With right sides together and using a ¼" (6 mm) seam allowance for all seams, sew the C piece to the D piece. Then sew on the E piece followed by the F piece. Press all seams to the side, toward the darker fabric.

6   Sew the G piece to the right side of the quilt center. Then sew one B piece to the right side of the quilt center and one B piece to the left side of the quilt center. Press the seams to the side, toward the darker fabric.

7   Sew the A piece to the top of the quilt center and the H piece to the bottom. Press the seams to the side.

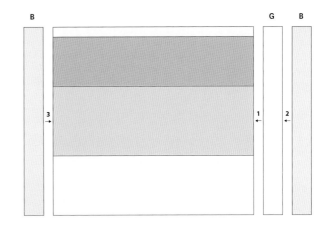

6   *Sewing the three vertical strips to the quilt center.*

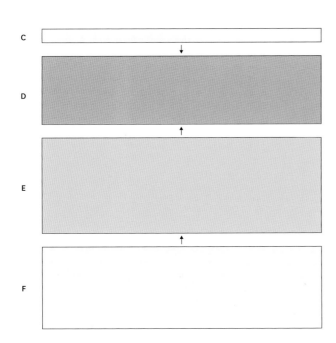

5   *Sewing together the four horizontal strips.*

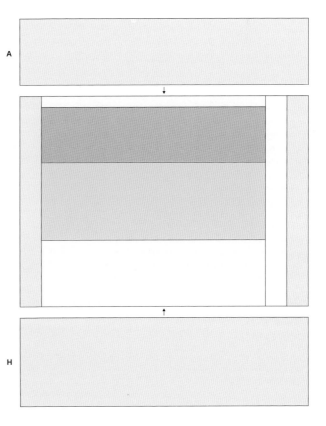

7   *Sewing on the top and bottom pieces.*

CUT AND PIECE THE QUILT BACK

8   To make the quilt back, cut two 62" (157.5 cm) x WOF pieces
    out of the backing fabric. Trimming off the selvages as you do
    so, trim each of the pieces *lengthwise* so that they measure
    37½" x 62" (95.5 cm x 157.5 cm). Sew the pieces right sides
    together, along one long edge, and press the seam allowances
    to the side.

FINISH THE QUILT

9   Layer the quilt top, batting, and quilt back to make a quilt
    sandwich (page 29). Baste together with quilting pins or
    basting stitches (page 30).

10 Quilt as desired (page 31). After quilting, trim off the excess
    batting and backing fabric to align them with the edges of the
    quilt top, and square up all sides of the quilt if necessary.

11 From the binding fabric, cut seven 2½" (6 cm) x WOF strips.
    Cut off the selvages and sew the seven strips together end-to-
    end to create the continuous binding strip (page 31). Bind the
    quilt as desired (page 33).

red lion

An old brick church in the town of Red Lion, Ohio, where my great grandparents got married in 1913, inspired this quilt. The church was built in 1853 and has these great large windows that easily measure ten feet tall. The four windows in the front are often covered by white wooden shutters. I love the contrast between the bright white of the painted slats of wood in the shutters and the brownish orange brickwork of the building, and that is what caught my attention when I set out to develop this quilt. I concentrated on one window of the church and explored the repetition of the linear white elements of the shutters, as well as the large white horizontal beams of the window sashing.

I chose a color palette similar to the actual church for the first version of Red Lion. Because I was focused on one shutter, I chose four shades of white to capture its subtleties—bright white, off-white, oyster, and cream. Three of these colors— the "darker" ones—are repeated throughout the two large pieced columns to recreate the linear element of the shutter, and I used the cooler bright white to represent the sashing that frames the shutter. To suggest the brickwork, I added two long vertical pieces of a warm brown woven plaid along the sides. The color palette of this version is primarily monochromatic, with variations of the color white, and the overall temperature of the palette is warm. The repetition of the strips in the patchwork columns creates a flow of movement up and down the quilt surface.

The second version of this project also has a primarily monochromatic color scheme, but with shades of pink in place of white. The pinks range from pale bubblegum to deeper medium pink. The colors vary in saturation, as the pale pink is muted while the medium pink is much more intense. I set the pink cottons against two shades of gray cotton, one of which is a very pale muted gray and the other a darker, more saturated gray, which I used in place of the brown in the first version. The temperature of this version is both warm and cool, as the grays are cool but the pinks are warm.

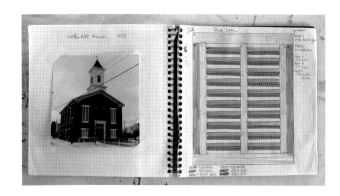

FINISHED QUILT SIZE

60½" x 74½" (151 cm x 186 cm)

FABRICS

The fabric amounts are based on using 44–45" (112–115 cm) wide fabrics.

COLORWAY 1
BROWN, WHITE, AND BEIGES

FABRIC 1: 2 yards (1.9 m) of a solid white, such as FreeSpirit *Designer Solids* in Winter White (S29)

FABRIC 2: 2 yards (1.9 m) of a simple brown plaid, such as Andover *Garden Gate Plaids* in Dark Earth (WV-5351-N)

FABRIC 3: 1 yard (92 cm) of a solid off-white, such as FreeSpirit *Designer Solids* in Pearl (S30)

FABRIC 4: ¾ yard (70 cm) of a solid pale oyster, such as FreeSpirit *Designer Solids* in Eggshell (S31)

FABRIC 5: ¾ yard (70 cm) of a solid pale cream, such as FreeSprit *Designer Solids* in Cream (S25)

BACKING FABRIC: 4 yards (3.7 m) more of Fabric 2

BINDING FABRIC: This is cut from the remainder of Fabric 2 (see step 2)

COLORWAY 2
GRAYS AND PINKS

FABRIC 1: 2 yards (1.9 m) of a solid pale gray, such as FreeSpirit *Designer Solids* in Pastel Gray (S97)

FABRIC 2: 2 yards (1.9 m) of a solid dark gray, such as FreeSpirit *Designer Solids* in Slate Gray (S99)

FABRIC 3: 1 yard (92 cm) of a solid pale pink, such as FreeSpirit *Designer Solids* in Rose (S22)

FABRIC 4: ¾ yard (70 cm) of a solid medium pink, such as FreeSpirit *Designer Solids* in Pink (S01)

FABRIC 5: ¾ yard (70 cm) of a solid dark pink, such as FreeSpirit *Designer Solids* in Cotton Candy (S57)

BACKING FABRIC: 4 yards (3.7 m) more of Fabric 2

BINDING FABRIC: This is cut from the remainder of Fabric 2 (see step 2)

OTHER MATERIALS

+ 65" x 79" (161 cm x 196 cm) piece of batting (or a twin-sized package)

+ All-purpose thread for piecing

+ Off-white quilting thread for colorway 1, OR pale pink for colorway 2

CUT THE QUILT-TOP PIECES

1 Using a rotary cutter, straight edge, and a cutting mat, cut one 62½" (156.2 cm) x width of fabric (WOF) piece from Fabric 1, cutting from selvage to selvage. Subcut this piece *lengthwise* into three 4½" x 62½" (11.2 cm x 156.2 cm) strips for three C pieces and two 6½" x 62½" (16.2 cm x 156.2 cm) strips. Trim the two 6½" x 62½" (16.2 cm x 156.2 cm) strips so that they each measure 6½" x 60½" (16.2 cm x 151.2 cm) for two A pieces. Pin a label to your pieces as you cut them.

2 From Fabric 2, cut one 62½" (156.2 cm) x WOF piece. Subcut this piece *lengthwise* into two 4½" x 62½" (11.2 cm x 156.2 cm) for two B pieces and five 2½" x 62½" (6.2 cm x 156.2 cm) strips for the binding. Set aside the binding strips to use in step 14.

3 From Fabric 3, cut eleven 2½" (6.2 cm) x WOF strips. Subcut each strip into two 2½" x 20½" (6.2 cm x 51.2 cm) strips to make 22 D pieces.

4 From Fabric 4, cut ten 2½" (6.2 cm) x WOF strips. Subcut each strip into two 2½" x 20½" (6.2 cm x 51.2 cm) strips to make 20 E pieces.

5 From Fabric 5, cut ten 2½" (6.2 cm) x WOF strips. Subcut each strip into two 2½" x 20½" (6.2 cm x 51.2 cm) strips to make 20 F pieces.

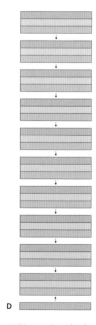

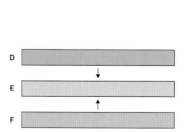

6 *Making the three-strip sets.*   7 *Making a pieced column.*

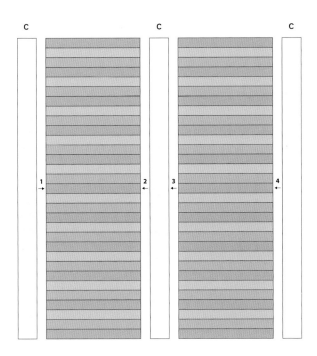

9   *Sewing the inner vertical strips to the pieced columns.*

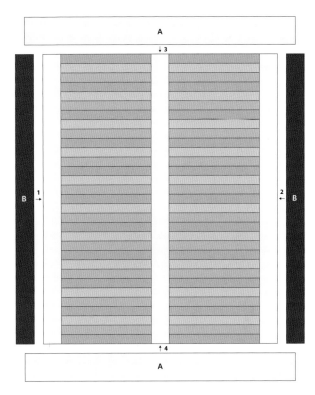

10 *Adding the outside borders.*

CONSTRUCT THE QUILT TOP

6   Following the diagram, sew the short strips together into three-strip sets. With right sides together and using a ¼" (6 mm) seam allowance for all seams, sew one D strip to one E strip, then add on one F strip to create one three-strip set. Press all seams to the side. Create a total of 20 three-strip sets in this way. (You will use the two remaining D strips in the next two steps.)

7   Sew ten of the strip sets together to form a vertical column, then add one D strip to the bottom of the column.

8   Repeat step 7 to create the second pieced column for the quilt center.

9   Following the diagram, sew one C piece to each side of one pieced column. Sew the other pieced column to the center C piece, followed by the last C piece. Press all seams to the side, toward the C pieces.

10 Sew one B piece to each side of the pieced quilt center. Then sew one A piece to the top of the quilt and one to the bottom. Press all seams to the side, toward the darker fabric.

CUT AND PIECE THE QUILT BACK

11 To make the quilt back, cut two 68" (173 cm) x WOF pieces out of the backing fabric. Trim the selvages off of each of the pieces. Sew the pieces right sides together, along one long edge, and press the seam allowance to the side.

FINISH THE QUILT

12 Layer the quilt top, batting, and quilt back to make a quilt sandwich (page 29). Baste together with quilting pins or basting stitches (page 30).

13 Quilt as desired (page 31). After quilting, trim off the excess batting and backing fabric to align them with the edges of the quilt top, and square up all sides of the quilt if necessary.

14 Take the five 2½" x 62½" (6.2 cm x 156.2 cm) strips of Fabric 2 that were cut in step 2 and sew them together end-to-end to create the continuous binding strip (page 31). Bind the quilt as desired (page 33).

caesar creek

The idea for this quilt project came from a large dam-control tower on a flood-control lake in Caesar Creek State Park in Waynesville, Ohio, which was constructed in the 1970s by the US Army Corps of Engineers. I was drawn to the surface of the building, specifically the contrast between the concrete structure and the natural elements that surround it, and the horizontal lines along the surface of the concrete. The horizontal lines create tiers, and I wanted to explore that repetition in my quilt design. I was also intrigued by the design of the tier in the upper middle of the tower, where the two rectangles flank one center square.

My first color scheme for the quilt contrasts with the actual colors of the building. Initially I began to draw shades of red, white, and blue in my sketchbook so that was what I chose for the fabrics. I selected a solid red fabric that felt more cool than warm temperature-wise because it had blue undertones, and I paired it with a cool white for the horizontal bands that make up the sashing between the large red sections. For the patchwork near the quilt center, I introduced two shades of solid blue—aqua for the center square and turquoise for the two rectangles that flank the square. The white strips of sashing break up the large areas of red, and the extra strip of sashing running along the bottom of the quilt emphasizes the asymmetrical design. Because the blues are cooler in temperature—that is, they have more green in their hues as opposed to purple/red—and because red and green are complementary colors, they really pop against the red.

In the second color scheme of the quilt, I incorporated a beautiful geometric print. I wanted to explore how the geometry would change when I cut the fabric into thin strips for the sashing. I didn't worry about the print matching in each thin section of sashing because I actually like the shift that occurs—it adds more interest and movement to the overall design. The print is a linen/cotton blend with a slightly rough weave, and I used it as the starting point for the remaining three fabric colors. Prints often have color keys on their selvage, showing the colors used, making it easy to find coordinating colors (especially solids) that will work well with them. I chose a muted aqua blue in place of the red for this version, and a berry pink for the two small rectangles and a muted olive green for the square. The overall color palette is much cooler than in the first version.

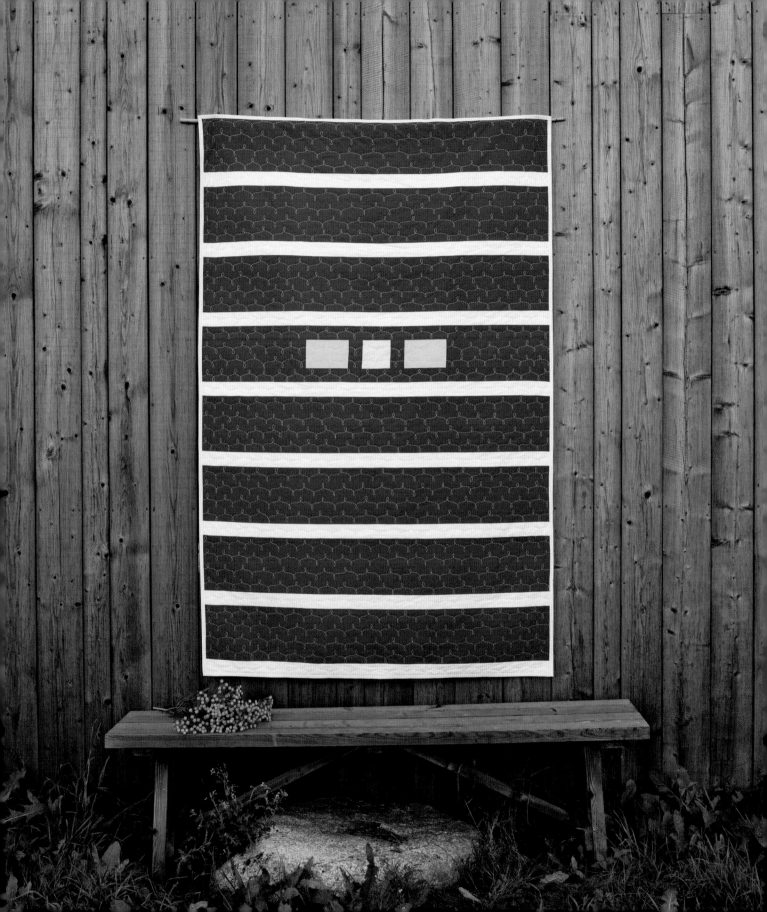

FINISHED QUILT SIZE

52½" x 80½" (133 cm x 201 cm)

FABRICS

The fabric amounts are based on using 44–45" (112–115 cm) wide fabrics.

COLORWAY 1
RED, WHITE, AND AQUA BLUES

FABRIC 1: 3 yards (2.8 m) of a solid red, such as Clothworks *American Made Brand Cotton Solids* in Dark Tomato (81)

FABRIC 2: 1½ yards (1.4 m) of a solid white, such as Clothworks *American Made Brand Cotton Solids* in White (01)

FABRIC 3: ¼ yard (25 cm) of a solid aqua blue, such as Clothworks *American Made Brand Cotton Solids* in Aqua (33)

FABRIC 4: ¼ yard (25 cm) of a solid light aqua blue, such as Clothworks *American Made Brand Cotton Solids* in Light Aqua (32)

BACKING FABRIC: 3½ yards (3.2 m) more of Fabric 3

BINDING FABRIC: ½ yard (50 cm) more of Fabric 2

COLORWAY 2
WHITE, MULTICOLORED PRINT, RASPBERRY, AND LIGHT GREEN

FABRIC 1: 3 yards (2.8 m) of a solid muted aqua such as FreeSpirit *Designer Solids* in Carribean Sea (S82)

FABRIC 2: 1½ yards (1.4 m) of a multicolored zigzag stripe print, such as Westminster Fabrics *Hapi Linen Sky Pyramid* by Amy Butler in Caramel

FABRIC 3: ¼ yard (25 cm) of a solid raspberry, such as Art Gallery Fabrics *Pure Elements* in Raspberry Rose (439)

FABRIC 4: ¼ yard (25 cm) of a solid light sage green, such as Robert Kaufman *Kona Cotton Solids* in Artichoke (347)

BACKING FABRIC: 3½ yards (3.2 m) of a solid bright light green, such as Robert Kaufman *Kona Cotton Solids* in Chartreuse (1072)

BINDING FABRIC: ½ yard (50 cm) more of Fabric 1

OTHER MATERIALS

+ 57" x 85" (143 cm x 211 cm) piece of batting (or a twin-sized package)

+ All-purpose thread for piecing

+ White quilting thread for colorway 1, OR off-white for colorway 2

CUT THE QUILT-TOP PIECES

1 Using a rotary cutter, straight edge, and a cutting mat, cut two 52½" (133.2 cm) x width of fabric (WOF) pieces from Fabric 1, cutting from selvage to selvage. Subcut the first piece *lengthwise* into four 8½" x 52½" (21.2 cm x 133.2 cm) strips for four A pieces and two 2½" x 52½" (6.2 cm x 133.2 cm) strips for two C pieces. Cut the second piece *lengthwise* into three 8½" x 52½" (21.2 cm x 133.2 cm) strips for the remaining three A pieces—for a total of seven A pieces. From the remaining Fabric 1, cut two 4½" x 16½" (11.2 cm x 42.2 cm) strips for two D pieces and two 2½" x 4½" (6.2 cm x 11.2 cm) rectangles for two F pieces. Pin a label to your pieces as you cut them.

2 From Fabric 2, cut one 52½" (133.2 cm) x WOF piece. Subcut this piece *lengthwise* into eight 2½" x 52½" (6.2 cm x 133.2 cm) strips for eight B pieces.

3 From Fabric 3, cut one 4½" (11.2 cm) x WOF strip. Subcut this strip into two 4½" x 6½" (11.2 cm x 16.2 cm) rectangles for two E pieces.

4 From Fabric 4, cut one 4½" (11.2 cm) x WOF strip. Subcut this strip into one 4½" x 4½" (11.2 cm x 11.2 cm) square for one G piece.

CONSTRUCT THE QUILT TOP

5 Following the diagram, construct the center section of the pieced stripe near the center of the quilt top. Sew one D piece to one E piece, with right sides together and using a ¼" (6 mm) seam allowance for all seams. Then sew on one F piece and one G piece, followed by the remaining F piece, the remaining E piece, and lastly the remaining D piece. Press all seams to the side, toward the darker fabric.

6 To complete the pieced stripe, sew one C piece to the top of the of the strip made in step 5 and one C piece to the bottom.

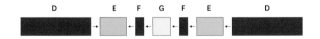

5 *Sewing together the center section of the pieced stripe.*

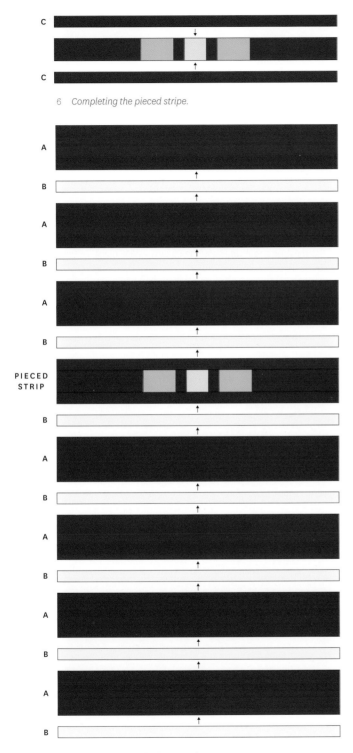

C

6 *Completing the pieced stripe.*

A

B

A

B

A

B

PIECED
STRIP

B

A

B

A

B

A

B

A

B

7 *Sewing together the horizontal stripes.*

7 Following the diagram from the top of the quilt, sew one A piece to one B piece. Then sew on one A piece, one B piece, one A piece, one B piece, and next the pieced stripe. Continue sewing on one B piece and one A piece alternately until one B piece remains. Finish by sewing on the last B piece. Press all seams to the side, toward the darker fabric.

CUT AND PIECE THE QUILT BACK

8 To make the quilt back, cut two 60" (152.5 cm) x WOF pieces out of the backing fabric. Trim the selvages off of each of the pieces. Sew the pieces right sides together, along one long edge, and press the seam allowance to the side.

FINISH THE QUILT

9 Layer the quilt top, batting, and quilt back to make a quilt sandwich (page 29). Baste together with quilting pins or basting stitches (page 30).

10 Quilt as desired (page 31). After quilting, trim off the excess batting and backing fabric to align them with the edges of the quilt top, and square up all sides of the quilt if necessary.

11 From the binding fabric, cut seven 2½" (6 cm) x WOF strips. Cut off the selvages and sew the seven strips together end-to-end to create the continuous binding (page 31). Bind the quilt as desired (page 33).

austin

I found the inspiration for this quilt only a few miles from my home—a metal storage building owned by the township. When I first saw the building I was transfixed by the linear look of the corrugated metal in varying lengths.

For version one, I chose jewel-toned colors that have differences in both intensity and value. The colors range from light pink to dark pink, a muted light lavender and a darker lavender, and a light blue and a darker, more saturated blue. The result is less harmonious and doesn't have the gentle flow of version two.

For version two, I created a harmonious color palette by combining blues and greens, which are analogous—they sit next to each other on the color wheel. The yellow hues add energy and movement. All of the colors in this version—two blues, two greens, and two yellows—are of a similar value, with a gradual, mellow shift in value from the "light" of the pale yellow to the "dark" of the medium blue.

FINISHED QUILT SIZE

Finished 44½" x 60½" (112 cm x 154 cm)

FABRICS

The fabric amounts are based on using 44-45" (112–115 cm) wide fabrics.

COLORWAY 1
PINKS, PURPLES, AND BLUES

FABRIC 1: ½ yard (50 cm) of a solid light pink, such as Clothworks *Everyday Organic Solids* in Y1074-41

FABRIC 2: ¾ yard (70 cm) of a solid rose pink, such as Clothworks *Everyday Organic Solids* in Y1215-43

FABRIC 3: ¾ yard (70 cm) of a solid pale purple-gray, such as Clothworks *Everyday Organic Solids* in Y0890-26

FABRIC 4: ¾ yard (70 cm) of a solid purple, such as Clothworks *Everyday Organic Solids* in Y1074-27

FABRIC 5: ¾ yard (70 cm) of a solid aqua, such as Clothworks *Everyday Organic Solids* in Y1074-29

FABRIC 6: ½ yard (50 cm) of a solid dark blue, such as Clothworks *Everyday Organic Solids* in Y1074-30

BACKING FABRIC: 3 yards (2.8 m) more of Fabric 5

BINDING FABRIC: ½ yard (50 cm) more of Fabric 5

COLORWAY 2
YELLOWS, GREENS, AND BLUES

FABRIC 1: ½ yard (50 cm) of a solid pale yellow, such as Robert Kaufman *Kona Cotton Solids* in Banana (1481)

FABRIC 2: ¾ yard (70 cm) of a solid medium yellow, such as Robert Kaufman *Kona Cotton Solids* in Daffodil (148)

FABRIC 3: ¾ yard (70 cm) of a solid light green, such as Robert Kaufman *Kona Cotton Solids* in Sprout (254)

FABRIC 4: ¾ yard (70 cm) of a solid blue-green, such as Robert Kaufman *Kona Cotton Solids* in Cypress (1474)

FABRIC 5: ¾ yard (70 cm) of a solid turquoise, such as Robert Kaufman *Kona Cotton Solids* in Capri (442)

FABRIC 6: ½ yard (50 cm) of a solid medium blue, such as Robert Kaufman *Kona Cotton Solids* in Lagoon (139)

BACKING FABRIC: 3 yards (2.8 m) of a solid light gray, such as Robert Kaufman *Kona Cotton Solids* in Silver (1333)

BINDING FABRIC: ½ yard (50 cm) of a solid light gray, such as Robert Kaufman *Kona Cotton Solids* in Silver (1333)

OTHER MATERIALS

+ 49" x 65" (122 cm x 164 cm) piece of batting (or a twin-sized package)

+ All-purpose thread for piecing

+ White quilting thread for both colorways

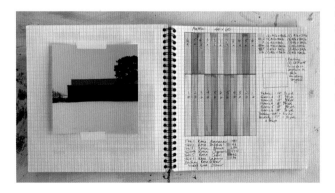

CUT THE QUILT-TOP PIECES

1   Using a rotary cutter, straight edge, and a cutting mat, cut three 4½" (11.2 cm) x width of fabric (WOF) strips from Fabric 1, cutting selvage to selvage. Trim one of these strips to 4½" x 24½" (11.2 cm x 62.2 cm) to make one 1a piece, and trim the remaining two strips to 4½" x 36½" (11.2 cm x 92.7 cm) to make two 1b pieces. Pin a label to your pieces as you cut them.

2   From Fabric 2, cut four 4½" (11.2 cm) x WOF strips. Trim two of these strips to 4½" x 24½" (11.2 cm x 62.2 cm) to make two 2a pieces, and trim the remaining two strips to 4½" x 36½" (11.2 cm x 92.7 cm) to make two 2b pieces.

3   From Fabric 3, cut four 4½" (11.2 cm) x WOF strips. Trim two of these strips to 4½" x 24½" (11.2 cm x 62.2 cm) to make two 3a pieces, and trim the remaining two strips to 4½" x 36½" (11.2 cm x 92.7 cm) to make two 3b pieces.

4   From Fabric 4, cut four 4½" (11.2 cm) x WOF strips. Trim two of these strips to 4½" x 24½" (11.2 cm x 62.2 cm) to make two 4a pieces, and trim the remaining two strips to 4½" x 36½" (11.2 cm x 92.7 cm) to make two 4b pieces.

5   From Fabric 5, cut four 4½" (11.2 cm) x WOF strips. Trim two of these strips to 4½" x 24½" (11.2 cm x 62.2 cm) to make two 5a pieces, and trim the remaining two strips to 4½" x 36½" (11.2 cm x 92.7 cm) to make two 5b pieces.

6   From Fabric 6, cut three 4½" (11.2 cm) x WOF strips. Trim two of these strips to 4½" x 24½" (11.2 cm x 62.2 cm) to make two 6a pieces, and trim the remaining strip to 4½" x 36½" (11.2 cm x 92.7 cm) to make one 6b piece.

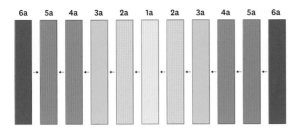

7   *Sewing together the top half of the quilt.*

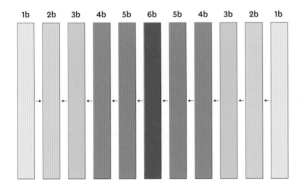

8   *Sewing together the bottom half of the quilt.*

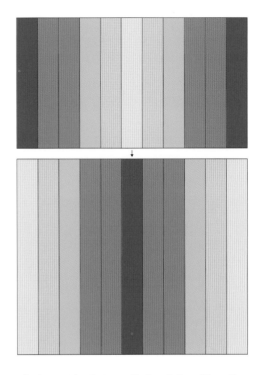

9   *Sewing together the top and bottom halves of the quilt.*

CONSTRUCT THE QUILT TOP

7   Following the diagram, sew one 6a piece to one 5a piece, with right sides together and using a ¼" (6 mm) seam allowance for all seams. Then sew on one 4a piece, one 3a piece, one 2a piece, one 1a piece, the second 2a piece, the second 3a piece, the second 4a piece, the second 5a piece, and finally the second 6a piece. Press all seams to the side, toward the darker fabrics, and set the top half of the quilt aside.

8   For the bottom half of the quilt, sew one 1b piece to one 2b piece. Then sew on one 3b piece, one 4b piece, one 5b piece, one 6b piece, the second 5b piece, the second 4b piece, the second 3b piece, the second 2b piece, and finally the second 1b piece. Press all seams to the side, toward the darker fabrics.

9   Sew the top half of the quilt top to the bottom half of the quilt top. Nest the seams between each seam of the top and bottom half. Press the seam open.

CUT AND PIECE THE QUILT BACK

10   To make the quilt back, cut two 52" (133 cm) x WOF pieces out of the backing fabric. Trimming off the selvages as you do so, trim each of the strips *lengthwise* so that they measure 34½" x 52" (88 cm x 133 cm). Sew the pieces right sides together, along one long edge, and press the seam allowances to the side.

FINISH THE QUILT

11   Layer the quilt top, batting, and quilt back to make a quilt sandwich (page 29). Baste together with quilting pins or basting stitches (page 30).

12   Quilt as desired (page 31). Trim off any excess batting and backing fabric to align them with the edges of the quilt top, and square up all sides of the quilt if necessary.

13   From the binding fabric, cut six 2½" (6 cm) x WOF strips. Cut off the selvedges and sew the six strips together end-to-end to create the binding (page 31). Bind the quilt as desired (page 33).

eden park

The design of this small wall hanging was inspired by tile work on the staircase of the Great Hall at the Cincinnati Art Museum. I used to work at the museum, so I have seen the staircase hundreds of times, but it wasn't until recently that I looked at the tiles up close and really paid attention to their rectangular shape, linear arrangement, and color shifts (most of the tiles are warm shades of gray and tan, but one has a much more yellow tone). While the staircase in the Great Hall is quite large, I focused on only a small section for my quilt. I have written the instructions so that you can either follow the exact placement of fabric "tiles" as I did, or you can lay each row out in a different order.

The first version of this quilt has a cool color palette, and I included a printed fabric along with three shades of solid blues—an aqua, a muted turquoise, and a saturated deep blue. For the thin sashing framework, I chose a bright white. The print is an abstract floral medallion design that I think works well with all of the blue solids. The blue solids don't match the blues in the print, but that doesn't bother me. In fact, because it is different, the printed rectangle draws the eye and adds visual interest just like the single yellow tile does at the museum. The overall color palette of this version is cool in temperature, as blue is a cool color, and it also verges on monochromatic with the repetition of shades and tints of blue.

The colors in the second version of the quilt are very similar to the actual colors of the inspiration. I used neutral, solid-colored cottons in three variations of cream and tan, which echo the stone tiles in the museum. The colors of the fabric are very similar to each other as well, with only slight variations in hue and value, with one being a bit lighter than the other two. I paired these neutrals with a solid curry yellow cotton to imitate the yellow tile in my inspiration. To represent the grout work in the staircase, I used a dark gray for the thin sashing framework. The overall color palette of this version is neutral, with a warm color temperature.

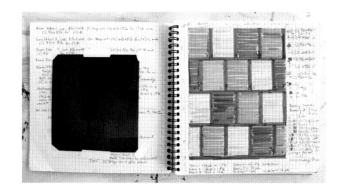

FINISHED QUILT SIZE

26½" x 34½" (66.5 cm x 86.5 cm)

FABRICS

The fabric amounts are based on using 44–45" (112–115 cm) wide fabrics.

COLORWAY 1

BLUES, WITH WHITE SASHING

FABRIC 1: ¼ yard (25 cm) of a solid dark blue, such as Robert Kaufman *Kona Cotton Solids* in Windsor (1389)

FABRIC 2: ¼ yard (25 cm) of a solid medium turquoise, such as Robert Kaufman *Kona Cotton Solids* in Breakers (440)

FABRIC 3: ¼ yard (25 cm) of a solid light blue, such as FreeSpirit *Designer Solids* in Sky (S14)

FABRIC 4: 10" (25 cm) square of a fabric print in aquamarine and blues, such as FreeSpirit *True Colors—Medallion* by Anna Maria Horner in Aquamarine

FABRIC 5: ¼ yard (25 cm) of a solid white, such as FreeSpirit *Designer Solids* in Artic White (S28)

BACKING FABRIC: 1 yard (92 cm) more of Fabric 5

BINDING FABRIC: ⅓ yard (35 cm) more of Fabric 5

COLORWAY 2

BEIGES AND YELLOW, WITH CHARCOAL SASHING

FABRIC 1: ¼ yard (25 cm) of a solid light brown, such as Robert Kaufman *Kona Cotton Solids* in Tan (1369)

FABRIC 2: ¼ yard (25 cm) of a solid light beige, such as Robert Kaufman *Kona Cotton Solids* in Sand (1323)

FABRIC 3: ¼ yard (25 cm) of a solid beige, such as Robert Kaufman *Kona Cotton Solids* in Khaki (1187)

FABRIC 4: 10" (25 cm) square of a solid mustard, such as Robert Kaufman *Kona Cotton Solids* in Curry (1677)

FABRIC 5: ¼ yard (25 cm) of a solid charcoal, such as Moda *Bella Solids* in Etchings Charcoal (171)

BACKING FABRIC: 1 yard (92 cm) more of Fabric 5

BINDING FABRIC: ⅓ yard (35 cm) more of Fabric 5

OTHER MATERIALS

+ 30" x 38" (74 cm x 84 cm) piece of batting

+ All-purpose thread for piecing

+ White quilting thread for colorway 1, OR beige for colorway 2

CUT THE QUILT-TOP PIECES

1 Using a rotary cutter, straight edge, and a cutting mat, cut one 8½" (21.2 cm) x width of fabric (WOF) strip from Fabric 1, cutting from selvage to selvage. Subcut this strip into five 6½" x 8½" (16.2 cm x 21.2 cm) pieces for five A pieces and one 3½" x 8½" (8.7 cm x 21.2 cm) piece for one B piece.

2 From Fabric 2, cut one 8½" (21.2 cm) x WOF strip. Subcut this strip into five 6½" x 8½" (16.2 cm x 21.2 cm) pieces for five C pieces and one 3½" x 8½" (8.7 cm x 21.2 cm) piece for one D piece.

3 From Fabric 3, cut one 8½" (21.2 cm) x WOF strip. Subcut this strip into three 6½" x 8½" (16.2 cm x 21.2 cm) pieces for three E pieces and two 3½" x 8½" (8.7 cm x 21.2 cm) pieces for two F pieces.

4 From Fabric 4, cut a piece that measures 6½" x 8½" (16.2 cm x 21.2 cm) for one G piece.

5 From Fabric 5, cut seven 1" (2.5 cm) x WOF strips. Subcut each of four of these strips into one 1" x 26½" (2.5 cm x 66.5 cm) strip and one 1" x 8½" (2.5 cm x 21.2 cm) strip, for a total of four J pieces and four H pieces. Subcut each of the remaining three 1" (2.5 cm) x WOF strips into four 1" x 8½" (2.5 cm x 21.2 cm) strips to make the remaining 12 H strips for a total of 16 H pieces.

CONSTRUCT THE QUILT TOP

6 Either arrange the full rectangles (A, C, and E pieces) and half rectangles (B, D, and F pieces) in exactly the sequence explained in steps 6–10, or make your own arrangement, laying the rectangles out on the floor in four rows following the diagrams in steps 6–9 until you have an arrangement you like. Construct row 1 at the top of the quilt first. Sew one full rectangle to one H piece, with right sides together and using a ¼" (6 mm) seam allowance for all seams. Following the diagram, add on another full rectangle, an H piece, another full rectangle, an H piece, a fourth full rectangle, and lastly another H piece to complete row 1 at the top of the quilt. Press all seams open.

7 Following the quilt layout diagram, sew one half rectangle to one H piece. Then add on a full rectangle, an H piece, another full rectangle, an H piece, a third full rectangle, an H piece, and lastly another half rectangle to complete row 2 of the quilt. Press all seams open.

8 Following the quilt layout diagram and using four full rectangles and four H pieces, construct row 3 in the same way as row 1 in step 6. Press all seams open.

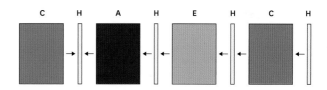

6   Sewing together row 1.

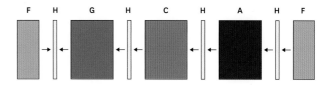

7   Sewing together row 2.

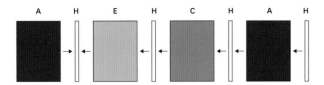

8   *Sewing together row 3.*

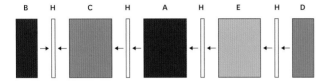

9   *Sewing together row 4.*

9   Following the quilt layout diagram and using two half rectangles, three full rectangles, and four H pieces, construct row 4 in the same way as row 2 in step 7. Press all seams open.

10 Following the quilt layout diagram, sew row 1 to one J piece. Then add on row 2, one J piece, row 3, one J piece, row 4, and lastly one J piece to complete the quilt top. Press all seams open.

CUT THE QUILT BACK

11 To make the quilt back, cut a 34" (86 cm) x WOF piece out of the backing fabric and trim off the selvages.

FINISH THE QUILT

12 Layer the quilt top, batting, and quilt back to make a quilt sandwich (page 29). Baste together with quilting pins or basting stitches (page 30).

13 Quilt as desired (page 31). After quilting, trim off the excess batting and backing fabric to align them with the edges of the quilt top, and square up all sides of the quilt if necessary.

14 From the binding fabric, cut four 2½" (6 cm) x WOF strips. Cut off the selvages and sew the four strips together end-to-end to create the continuous binding (page 31). Bind the quilt as desired (page 33).

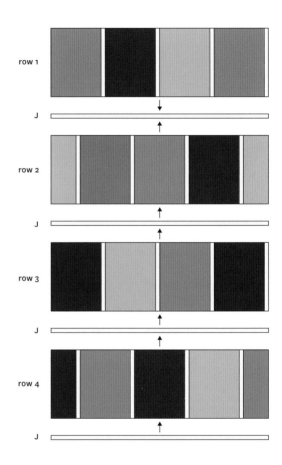

10 *Completing the quilt top.*

third street

The asymmetrical grid on the back wall of an abandoned building on Third Street in down-town Dayton, Ohio, inspired the design of this minimalist quilt. I don't know the history of the grid, but it could be a remnant of another building that used to stand next to this one. I love how the grid changes in size—especially toward the bottom—how the negative space is more pronounced on the right side, and the strong graphic contrast between its creamy white color and the reddish brown brickwork around it.

For the first version, which is similar to the inspiration, I used two colors of a yarn-dyed cotton-linen blend fabric: a warm tannish brown and a creawmy white. I chose this fabric because its coarse weave and the way it's dyed make the colors look less flat than conventionally dyed cotton. I love how the cooler cream pops against the brown so that the grid appears quite crisp against the tan negative space (background).

For the second version, I chose two colors that sit directly across from each other on the color wheel—turquoise and red-orange—in the same linen-cotton blend fabric. Because turquoise is a tint/variation of blue, and orange is the complement of blue, these two colors vibrate against each other. While two complementary colors can sometimes be tricky to use together, and sometimes clash with each other, they work well here because the amount of red-orange is limited, so while the orange is a more intense color, it doesn't overpower the composition. The limited saturation in this particular hue of orange also helps subdue a clash.

FINISHED QUILT SIZE

56½" x 72½" (142 cm x 182 cm)

FABRICS

The fabric amounts are based on using 44-45" (112-115 cm) wide fabrics.

COLORWAY 1
BROWN AND WHITE

FABRIC 1: 3 yards (2.8 m) of a solid brown, such as Robert Kaufman *Essex* linen/cotton blend in Taupe (1371)

FABRIC 2: 1 yard (92 cm) of a solid cream, such as Robert Kaufman *Essex* linen/cotton blend in Linen (308)

BACKING FABRIC: 3¾ yards (3.5 m) more of Fabric 1

BINDING FABRIC: ½ yard (50 cm) more of Fabric 1

COLORWAY 2
TURQUOISE AND ORANGE

FABRIC 1: 3 yards (2.8 m) of a solid turquoise, such as Robert Kaufman *Essex* linen/cotton blend in Medium Aqua (1221)

FABRIC 2: 1 yard (92 cm) of a solid orange, such as Robert Kaufman *Essex* linen/cotton blend in Orange (1265)

BACKING FABRIC: 3¾ yards (3.5 m) more of Fabric 1

BINDING FABRIC: ½ yard (50 cm) more of Fabric 1

OTHER MATERIALS

+ 61" x 77" (152 cm x 192 cm) piece of batting (or a twin-sized package)

+ All-purpose thread for piecing

+ Cream quilting thread for colorway 1, OR turquoise for colorway 2

CUT THE QUILT-TOP PIECES

1 Using a rotary cutter, straight edge, and a cutting mat, cut one 75" (190 cm) x width of fabric (WOF) piece from Fabric 1, cutting from selvage to selvage. Subcut this piece *lengthwise* into one 20½" x 75" (52.2 cm x 190 cm) rectangle and one 16½" x 75" (41.2 cm x 190 cm) strip. Trim the larger rectangle to 20½" x 72½" (52.2 cm x 181.7 cm) for one H piece. Subcut the 16½" x 75" (41.2 cm x 190 cm) strip into two 4½" x 16½" (11.2 cm x 41.2 cm) rectangles for two D pieces, two 14½" x 16½" (36.7 cm x 41.2 cm) rectangles for two F pieces, and four 8½" x 16½" (21.2 cm x 41.2 cm) rectangles for four B pieces. Pin a label to your pieces as you cut them.

2 From Fabric 1, cut three 8½" (21.2 cm) x WOF strips. Subcut each of these strips into two 8½" x 16½" (21.2 cm x 41.2 cm) rectangles to make the remaining six B pieces. You will now have a total of ten B pieces.

3 From Fabric 2, cut seven 2½" (6.2 cm) x WOF strips. Trim each of these strips to 2½" x 36½" (6.2 cm x 91.2 cm) for seven A pieces.

4 From Fabric 2, cut three 2½" (6.2 cm) x WOF strips. Subcut each of two of these strips into four 2½" x 8½" (6.2 cm x 21.2 cm) strips and the third strip into two 2½" x 8½" (6.2 cm x 21.2 cm) strips for a total of ten C pieces.

5 From Fabric 2, cut one 2½" (6.2 cm) x WOF strip. Subcut this strip into two 2½" x 14½" (6.2 cm x 36.7 cm) strips for two G pieces and two 2½" x 4½" (6.2 cm x 11.2 cm) strips for two E pieces.

CONSTRUCT THE QUILT TOP

6 Following the diagram, construct a pieced section with two B pieces and two C Pieces. Sew one B piece to one C piece, right sides together and using a ¼" (6 mm) seam allowance for all seams. Sew on another B piece and another C piece to complete the first B/C/B/C section. Press all seams to the side, toward the darker fabric. Repeat this step four more times for a total of five pieced B/C/B/C sections that are rows 1–5 of the quilt top.

7 Following the diagram, sew one D piece to one E piece. Then add on another D piece and another E piece. Press all seams to the side, toward the darker fabric. This is row 6 of the quilt top.

8 Following the diagram, sew one F piece to one G piece. Sew on another F piece and another G piece. Press all seams to the side, toward the darker fabric. This is Row 7 of the quilt top.

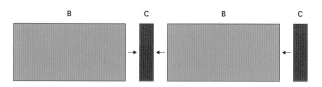

6   *Sewing together the B/C/B/C sections.*

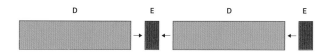

7   *Sewing together the D/E/D/E section.*

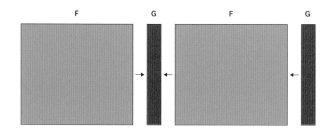

8   *Sewing together the F/G/F/G section.*

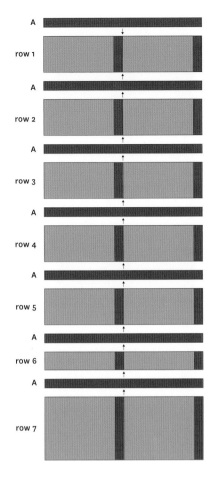

9   *Sewing together the horizontal rows.*

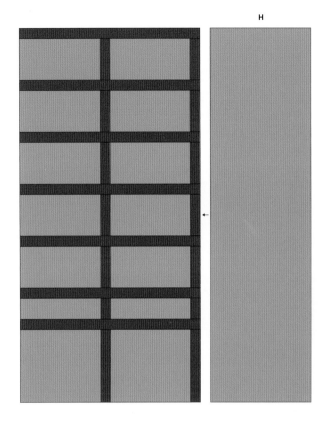

10 *Completing the quilt top.*

9   Following the diagram, sew together rows 1–7 and seven A
    pieces. Beginning at the top, sew one A piece to the top of row
    1 and one A piece to the bottom of row 1. Continue adding on
    one row and one A piece alternately, ending with row 7. Press all
    seams to the side, toward the darker fabric.

10 Sew the H piece to the right side edge of the pieced section,
    following the diagram. Press the seam allowances to the side,
    toward the darker fabric.

CUT AND PIECE THE QUILT BACK

11 To make the quilt back, cut two 64" (162.5 cm) x WOF pieces out
    of the backing fabric. Trim the selvages off of each of the pieces.
    Sew the pieces right sides together, along one long edge, and
    press the seam allowance to the side.

FINISH THE QUILT

12 Layer the quilt top, batting, and quilt back to make a quilt
    sandwich (page 29). Baste together with quilting pins or basting
    stitches (page 30).

13 Quilt as desired (page 31). After quilting, trim off the excess
    batting and backing fabric to align them with the edges of the
    quilt top, and square up all sides of the quilt if necessary.

14 From the binding fabric, cut seven 2½" (6 cm) x WOF strips. Cut
    off the selvages and sew the seven strips together end-to-end to
    create the continuous binding (page 31). Bind the quilt as desired
    (page 33).

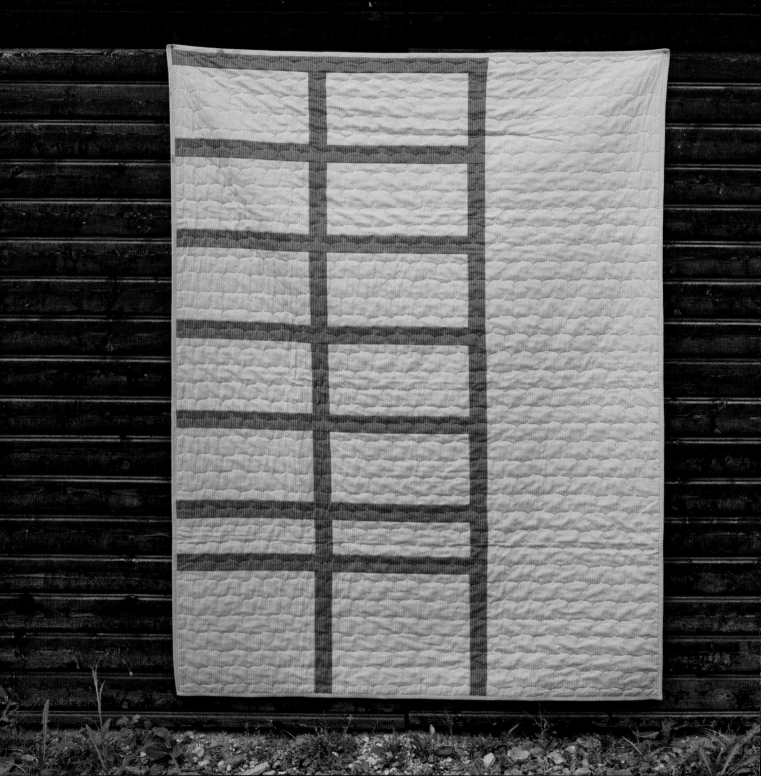

covington

SKILL LEVEL: INTERMEDIATE

This quilted pillow cover was inspired by Ascent, a residential building in Covington, Kentucky, just across the river from Cincinnati, which was designed by architect Daniel Libeskind and built in 2008. I love the strong graphic quality of the building and the geometric lines of the repetition of concrete and glass. The building has a very distinct curve along its roofline and ends in a sharp peak as it reaches toward the sky. For my design, I focused on the geometric and irregular linear pattern on a section of the building near the roofline. I used thin strips of fabric, and I included a triangle in the upper left section of the design to suggest the apex of the building.

The first version of the cover echoes the color palette of Ascent: a solid cobalt blue cotton and a solid white. The color combination gives the finished project a crisp feel because the blue is such a saturated color and the white a neutral with a lower value. The stark contrast between these two colors makes the graphic nature of the design very strong.

For the second version, I used a stripe-and-circle print combined with a solid peacock blue. I especially love the way the print looks when it is cut into thin strips, so I used it in place of the white in the first version. Even though the print is more visually complex than the white, it doesn't stand out as much. This is because there is not as strong a difference in value between the peacock blue and the print as there is between the white and cobalt blue.

FINISHED COVER SIZE
19½" x 19½" (49 cm x 49 cm)

FABRICS
The fabric amounts are based on using 44–45" (112–115 cm) wide fabrics.

COLORWAY 1
WHITE AND DARK BLUE

FABRIC 1: ½ yard (50 cm) of a solid white, such as Clothworks *American Made Brand Cotton Solids* in White (01)

FABRIC 2: ½ yard (50 cm) of a solid blue, such as Clothworks *American Made Brand Cotton Solids* in Dark Blue (30)

BACKING FABRIC FOR PILLOW-COVER FRONT: 26" (65 cm) square of white cotton fabric

FABRIC FOR PILLOW-COVER BACK: ½ yard (50 cm) more of Fabric 2

COLORWAY 2
MULTICOLORED PRINT AND BLUE

FABRIC 1: ½ yard (50 cm) of a multicolored print, such as Westminster Fibers *Hapi Glow* by Amy Butler in Linen

FABRIC 2: ½ yard (50 cm) of a solid blue, such as FreeSpirit *Designer Solids* in Rocket Blue (S72)

BACKING FABRIC FOR PILLOW-COVER FRONT: 26" (65 cm) square of white cotton fabric

FABRIC FOR PILLOW-COVER BACK: ½ yard (50 cm) more of Fabric 1

OTHER MATERIALS
+ 24" x 24" (60 cm x 60 cm) of batting
+ All-purpose thread for piecing and sewing cover together
+ White quilting thread for colorway 1, OR off-white for colorway 2
+ 20" x 20" (50 cm x 50 cm) premade pillow form

CUT THE PILLOW-COVER TOP PIECES

1   Using a rotary cutter, straight edge, and a cutting mat, cut three 1½" (3.7 cm) x width of fabric (WOF) strips from Fabric 1, cutting from selvage to selvage. Pinning labels to all pieces as you cut them, subcut the first strip into the following pieces:

> 1½" x 3½" (3.7 cm x 8.7 cm) for the E piece
> 1½" x 9½" (3.7 cm x 23.7 cm) for the G piece
> 1½" x 11½" (3.7 cm x 28.7 cm) for the H piece
> 1½" x 9½" (3.7 cm x 23.7 cm) for the M piece
> From the second strip, subcut the following pieces:
> 1½" x 20½" (3.7 cm x 51.2 cm) for the K piece
> 1½" x 7½" (3.7 cm x 18.7 cm) for the O piece
> 1½" x 11½" (3.7 cm x 28.7 cm) for the R piece
> From the third strip, subcut the following pieces:
> 1½" x 8½" (3.7 cm x 21.2 cm) for the U piece
> 1½" x 9½" (3.7 cm x 23.7 cm) for the V piece
> 1½" x 2½" (3.7 cm x 6.2 cm) for the Y piece
> 1½" x 5½" (3.7 cm x 13.7 cm) for the Z piece

2   From Fabric 1, cut one 3½" (8.7 cm) x WOF strip. Trim this strip into the following piece:

> 3½" x 20½" (8.7 cm x 51.2 cm) for the A piece

3   From Fabric 1, cut one 4" x 4" (10.2 cm x 10.2 cm) square for the B piece (to use for making the B/C half-square-triangle square).

4   From Fabric 2, cut two 1½" (3.7 cm) x WOF strips. Subcut the first strip into the following pieces:

> 1½" x 3½" (3.7 cm x 8.7 cm) for the F piece
> 1½" x 11½" (3.7 cm x 28.7 cm) for the L piece
> 1½" x 2½" (3.7 cm x 6.2 cm) for the N piece
> 1½" x 11½" (3.7 cm x 28.7 cm) for the P piece
> 1½" x 4½" (3.7 cm x 11.2 cm) for the Q piece
> 1½" x 5½" (3.7 cm x 13.7 cm) for the S piece

> From the second strip, subcut the following pieces:
> 1½" x 1½" (3.7 cm x 3.7 cm) for the T piece
> 1½" x 3½" (3.7 cm x 8.7 cm) for the X piece

5   From Fabric 2, cut two 2½" (6.2 cm) x WOF strips. Subcut the first strip into the following pieces.

> 2½" x 6½" (6.2 cm x 16.2 cm) for the D piece
> 2½" x 20½" (6.2 cm x 51.2 cm) for the MM piece
> 2½" x 11½" (6.2 cm x 28.7 cm) for the W piece

> Trim the second strip into the following piece:
> 2½" x 15½" (6.2 cm x 38.7 cm) for the ZZ piece

6   From Fabric 2, cut one 3½" (8.7 cm) x WOF strip. Subcut this strip into the following pieces:

> 3½" x 8½" (8.7 cm x 21.2 cm) for the CC piece
> 3½" x 11½" (8.7 cm x 28.2 cm) for the J piece

7   From Fabric 2, cut one 4½" (11.2 cm) x WOF strip. Subcut this strip into the following pieces:

> 4½" x 9½" (11.2 cm x 23.7 cm) for the JJ piece
> 4" x 4" (10.2 cm x 10.2 cm) square for the C piece (to use for making the B/C half-square-triangle square)

CONSTRUCT THE PILLOW-COVER FRONT TOP

8   Using the 4" (10.2 cm) B and C squares, make a half-square-triangle square following steps 10–13 for the Franklin No. 2 quilt (page 72). You will only need one of the pieced squares for this pillow cover, so add the second pieced square to your scrap bin. Press the seam allowance on the B/C pieced square to the side, toward the darker fabric. Square up the square so that it measures 3½" x 3½" (8.7 cm x 8.7 cm) if necessary.

9   Following the diagram, construct column 2 from the B/C square and the CC, D, E, F, and G pieces. Sew the pieces with right sides together and using a ¼" (6 mm) seam allowance for all seams. Sew the pieces together in the order shown, pressing the seam open after sewing each seam.

10 Following the diagram, construct column 3 from the H, J, and JJ pieces. Sew the pieces together in the order shown, pressing the seam open after sewing each seam.

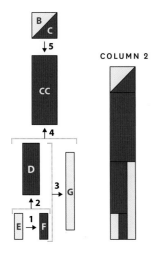

COLUMN 2

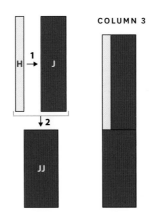

COLUMN 3

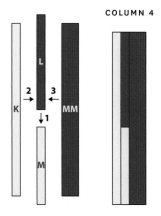

COLUMN 4

9 *Sewing together column 2.*

10 *Sewing together column 3.*

11 *Sewing together column 4.*

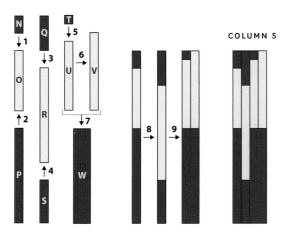

COLUMN 5

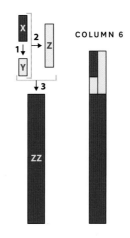

COLUMN 6

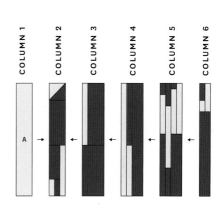

12 *Sewing together column 5*

13 *Sewing together column 6.*

14 *Sewing together the columns to complete the top.*

11 Following the diagram, construct column 4 from the K, L, M, and MM pieces. Sew the pieces together in the order shown, pressing the seam open after sewing each seam.

12 Following the diagram, construct column 5 from the N, O, P, Q, R, S, T, U, V, and W pieces. Sew the pieces together in the order shown, sewing together three vertical pieced sections first as shown (arrows 1–7), then sewing together these three sections (arrows 8 and 9). Press the seam open after sewing each seam.

13 Following the diagram, construct column 6 from the X, Y, Z, and ZZ pieces. Sew the pieces together in the order shown, pressing the seam open after sewing each seam.

14 Sew column 1 (the A piece) to pieced column 2. Then sew on pieced columns 3, 4, 5, and 6 following the diagram to complete the pillow-cover front top.

FINISH THE PILLOW-COVER FRONT

15 Layer the batting between the pillow-cover front top and the 26" (65 cm) square of backing fabric to make a quilt sandwich (page 29). Baste together with quilting pins (page 30).

16 Quilt as desired (page 31). After quilting, trim off the excess batting and backing fabric to align them with the edges of the pillow-cover front top, and square up all sides of the quilted piece if necessary.

SEW ON THE PILLOW-COVER BACK

17 First, cut one 15½" (38.7 cm) x WOF strip from the pillow-cover back fabric. Subcut this strip into two 15½" x 20½" (38.7 cm x 51.2 cm) rectangles for the two back pieces.

18 Fold and press ½" (12 mm) then 1½" (3.8 cm) to the wrong side along one long edge of one back piece to create a double hem. Repeat on the second back piece. Pin both hems in place and machine stitch each hem close to the second fold.

19 Place the back pieces on a flat surface, wrong side up, and overlap the hemmed edges at the center as shown so that they form a 20½" (51.2 cm) square—the same size as the pillow-cover front. Pin the two pieces together along the one hemmed edge using straight pins or quilting pins, then machine stitch the two pieces together where they overlap along the outside edges, stitching ¼" (6 mm) from the edge, to create one backing piece.

20 Place the pillow-cover front on top of the pillow-cover back, with right sides together, and pin in place. Keep the pins on the back to stabilize the envelope section during this step. Using a ½" (12 mm) seam allowance, start stitching all around perimeter of the pillow square. At the first corner, stop the sewing machine ½" (12 mm) from the next side edge, with the needle down. Then lift the presser foot of the machine, pivot the fabric 90 degrees counterclockwise, lower the presser foot, and continue to the next corner. Continue in this way until all four sides are joined together.

21 Snip off the seam allowance corners on the pillow cover, making sure to not cut the stitches of the seam. Finish the raw edges of the pillow cover by serging them or sewing them with a machine zigzag stitch. Remove the pins from the hem on the back and turn pillow cover right side out. Insert the premade pillow form.

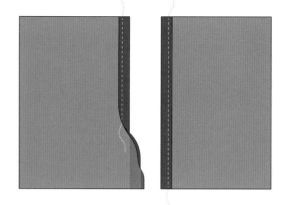

18 *Hemming the inside edges of the pillow-cover back pieces.*

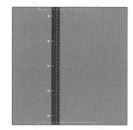

19 *Hemming the inside edges of the pillow-cover back pieces.*

20 *Sewing together the pillow-cover front and back.*

union terminal

The inspiration for this design was the ceiling of the rotunda at Union Terminal, an amazing Art Deco building constructed as a train station in Cincinnati, Ohio, in 1933. The building is currently known as the Museum Center (although it is still a train station, it also houses three different museums). The massive concrete structure features beautiful curvilinear lines inside and out. I explored the concentric rings in my quilt design by stacking three quarter-circles in various sizes on top of each other on a background square using raw-edge appliqué and a fusible adhesive webbing. This pattern is block-based, and I've written the instructions for a small quilt, but you can easily make the quilt a larger size by increasing the number of blocks.

In the first version, I recreated the actual palette of the ceiling. I used a solid medium yellow for the background square and built the concentric rings in dark taupe, orange, and light gray. I really love the negative space created when the blocks are sewn together. As yellow and orange sit next to each other on the color wheel, this color palette is an analogous one, and the dark taupe and light gray fabrics act as neutrals in the design. The overall temperature of this combination is warm.

I created a cool color palette for the second version with light purple, teal green, cream, and navy blue. Because the smallest quarter-circle is made out of the darkest fabric in the palette, and it is placed next to the lightest color, attention is naturally drawn to this section of the design.

36½" x 36½" (93 cm x 93 cm)

FABRICS

*The fabric amounts are based on
using 44–45" (112–115 cm) wide
fabrics.*

COLORWAY 1
YELLOW, GRAY, ORANGE, AND TAUPE

FABRIC 1: 1¼ yards (1.2 m) of a
solid yellow, such as Clothworks
*American Made Brand Cotton
Solids* in Dark Yellow (10)

FABRIC 2: ½ yard (50 cm) of a
solid light gray, such as Clothworks
*American Made Brand Cotton
Solids* in Light Gray (05)

FABRIC 3: ¾ yard (70 cm) of a
solid orange, such as Clothworks
*American Made Brand Cotton
Solids* in Orange (36)

FABRIC 4: 1 yard (92 cm) of a solid
dark taupe, such as Clothworks
*American Made Brand Cotton
Solids* in Dark Taupe (63)

BACKING FABRIC: 1¼ yards (1.2 m)
more of Fabric 4

BINDING FABRIC: ⅓ yard (35 cm)
more of Fabric 1

COLORWAY 2
BLUES, OFF-WHITE, AND TURQUOISE

FABRIC 1: 1¼ yards (1.2 m) of a
solid light blue, such as Clothworks
*American Made Brand Cotton
Solids* in Periwinkle (85)

FABRIC 2: ½ yard (50 cm) of a
solid dark blue, such as Clothworks
*American Made Brand Cotton
Solids* in Dark Indigo (96)

FABRIC 3: ¾ yard (70 cm) of a
solid off-white, such as Clothworks
*American Made Brand Cotton
Solids* in Light Cream (02)

FABRIC 4: 1 yard (92 cm) of a solid
turquoise, such as Clothworks
*American Made Brand Cotton
Solids* in Dark Turquoise (102)

BACKING FABRIC: 1¼ yards (1.2 m)
more of Fabric 2

BINDING FABRIC: ⅓ yard (35 cm)
more of Fabric 1

OTHER MATERIALS

+ 39" x 39" (100 cm x 100 cm) piece
of batting

+ 5 yards (5.5 m) of a heavy-duty
iron-on paper-backed fusible
adhesive webbing, 15" (38 cm)
wide—I used a 5 yard (5.5 m)
package of 15" (38 cm) wide
Pellon® *Heavy-Duty Wonder
Under*

+ All-purpose thread for piecing

+ Yellow quilting thread for colorway
1, OR off-white for colorway 2

CUT THE QUILT-TOP PIECES

1   Using a rotary cutter, straight edge, and a cutting mat, cut three
12½" (31.7 cm) x width of fabric (WOF) strips from Fabric 1,
cutting from selvage to selvage. Subcut each of the three strips
into three 12½" x 12½" (31.7 cm x 31.7 cm) squares, for a total of
nine A pieces.

PREPARE THE QUARTER-CIRCLE PIECES

2   Using a pencil, trace templates B, C, and D on page 156 nine
times each on the paper side of the fusible webbing, leaving
about ½" (12 mm) between the shapes. Cut out the traced
templates with a pair of scissors, cutting around the perimeter
of each drawn template—do not cut directly *on* the drawn
outlines of the template shapes, but rather leave about ¼"
(6 mm) around each shape. (Once the fusible-web template
shapes are fused onto the fabric, the fabric pieces will be cut
out precisely along the outlines.)

3   Following the manufacturer's directions, adhere the nine fusible
B template shapes to the wrong side of Fabric 2 with a hot iron.
Allow to cool and then cut out with a pair of scissors along the
drawn outline of each template shape.

4   Following the manufacturer's directions, adhere the nine fusible
C template shapes to the wrong side of Fabric 3 with a hot iron.
Allow to cool and then cut out with a pair of scissors along the
drawn outline of each template shape.

5   Following the manufacturer's directions, adhere the nine fusible
D template shapes to the wrong side of Fabric 4 with a hot iron.
Allow to cool and then cut out with a pair of scissors along the
drawn outline of each template shape.

MAKE THE QUILT BLOCKS

6   Peel off the paper backing of one D piece. Following the diagram,
place the D piece on top of one A square, aligning the straight
edges with the edges of the A square. Fuse the D piece in place
with a hot iron.

7   Peel off the paper backing of one C piece and place on top of the
D piece, aligning the straight edges. Fuse in place.

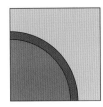

6 *Fusing the D piece to the fabric square.*

7 *Fusing the C piece in place.*

8 *Fusing the B piece in place.*

8 Peel off the paper backing of one B piece and place on top of the C piece, aligning the straight edges. Fuse in place.

9 Repeat steps 6–8 eight more times to create a total of nine quilt blocks.

CONSTRUCT THE QUILT TOP

10 Following the diagram, sew three blocks together to create row 1. Press all seams to the side, away from the fusible webbing. Repeat this step two more times to create rows 2 and 3.

11 Sew row 1 to row 2, following the diagram. Press the seams to the side, toward row 2. Sew row 3 to row 2, and press the seams to the side, toward row 3.

CUT THE QUILT BACK

12 To make the quilt back, cut a 44" (112 cm) x WOF piece out of the backing fabric. Remove the selvages.

FINISH THE QUILT

13 Layer the quilt top, batting, and quilt back to make a quilt sandwich (page 29). Baste together with quilting pins or basting stitches (page 30).

14 Quilt as desired (page 31). After quilting, trim off the excess batting and backing fabric to align them with the edges of the quilt top, and square up all sides of the quilt if necessary.

15 From the binding fabric, cut four 2½" (6 cm) x WOF strips. Cut off the selvages and sew the four strips together end-to-end to create the continuous binding (page 31). Bind the quilt as desired (page 33).

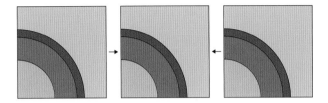

10 *Sewing the squares together in rows.*

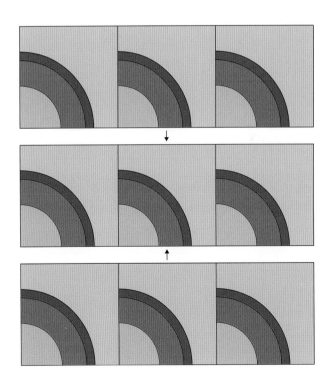

11 *Sewing together the rows to complete the quilt top.*

west chester

There are a number of nineteenth- and early-twentieth-century barns around my home that have text integrated into the construction of the roof, but I especially love the font used on the renovated nineteenth-century one in West Chester, Ohio, that inspired this quilt. It reads "G. Mulhauser 1881," and the large letters and numbers are constructed from roof tiles in a different color than the background; they are arranged in such a way that they can be read from quite a distance away. I chose the word "MAKE" for this quilt, but you could easily extend the alphabet and spell out anything you'd like in yours.

The background in the first version is a light-colored fabric, a natural cream, and the letters are a darker fabric—a solid blue. The blue is a muted hue that gives this quilt a vintage look, especially as it is paired with the natural-colored cotton. I chose to quilt West Chester in an organic figure-eight pattern, but the expansive negative space of this project would be great for experimenting with and showcasing your favorite free-motion quilting designs. The overall color palette is quite simple—I didn't want to use fabrics that would compete with the simplicity of the design of the quilt itself.

For the second version, I used darker colors. The background is dark gray and the pieced letters are mustard yellow. There is less overall contrast between the two colors in this version than in the first, because they are closer in value than the two that I used in the first version. Where the first version looks like it could have been the color palette of a vintage or much older quilt, these colors feel more modern together.

FINISHED QUILT SIZE

50½" x 70½" (131 cm x 181 cm)

FABRICS

The fabric amounts are based on using 44-45" (112-115 cm) wide fabrics.

COLORWAY 1
OFF-WHITE AND BLUE

FABRIC 1: 3¼ yards (3 m) of a solid off-white, such as FreeSpirit *Designer Solids* in Natural (S44)

FABRIC 2: ¼ yard (25 cm) of a solid dark blue, such as Robert Kaufman *Kona Cotton Solids* in Cadet (1058)

BACKING FABRIC: 3½ yards (3.2 m) of a solid dark red, such as Robert Kaufman *Kona Cotton Solids* in Cardinal (1063)

BINDING FABRIC: ½ yard (50 cm) more of Fabric 1

COLORWAY 2
GRAY AND GOLD

FABRIC 1: 3¼ yards (3 m) of a solid dark gray, such as Clothworks *American Made Brand Cotton Solids* in Dark Gray (07)

FABRIC 2: ¼ yard (25 cm) of a solid gold, such as Clothworks *American Made Brand Cotton Solids* in Dark Gold (69)

BACKING FABRIC: 3½ yards (3.2 m) of a solid light gray, such as Clothworks *American Made Brand Cotton Solids* in Light Gray (05)

BINDING FABRIC: ½ yard (50 cm) more of Fabric 1

OTHER MATERIALS

+ 55" x 75" (141 cm x 191 cm) piece of batting (or a twin-sized package)

+ All-purpose thread for piecing

+ Off-white quilting thread for for colorway 1, OR gray for colorway 2

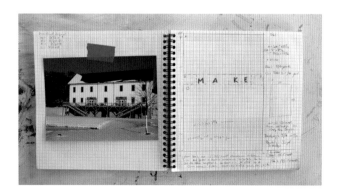

CUT THE QUILT TOP PIECES

1 Using a rotary cutter, straight edge, and a cutting mat, cut two 50½" (130.8 cm) x width of fabric (WOF) pieces from Fabric 1, cutting from selvage to selvage. Trim one piece so that it measures 40½" x 50½" (103 cm x 130.8 cm) for one C piece. Subcut the other piece *lengthwise* into one 24" x 50½" (61 cm x 130.8 cm) rectangle for one A piece, and from the remaining fabric cut two 7" x 7½" (18.1 cm x 19.2 cm) rectangles for two B pieces. Pin a label to these pieces as you cut them. (Set the A, B, and C pieces aside while you make the letter blocks.)

2 From Fabric 1, cut twelve 1" (2.5 cm) x WOF strips. These strips will be cut to make the pieces for the background on the letter blocks.

3 From Fabric 2, cut seven 1" (2.5 cm) x WOF strips. These strips will be cut to make the pieces for the letters on the letter blocks.

CUT AND PIECE LETTER BLOCK "M"

4 To make letter block "M," you will need three of the 1" (2.5 cm) x WOF strips of Fabric 1 and two of the 1" (2.5 cm) x WOF strips of Fabric 2. From the first Fabric 1 strip, cut the following pieces:

12 D pieces, each 1" x 1" (2.5 cm x 2.5 cm)
15 E pieces, each 1" x 1½" (2.5 cm x 3.8 cm)
2 G pieces, each 1" x 2½" (2.5 cm x 6.4 cm)

From the second Fabric 1 strip, cut the following pieces:
1 G piece, 1" x 2½" (2.5 cm x 6.4 cm)
1 J piece, 1" x 3½" (2.5 cm x 9 cm)
4 L pieces, each 1" x 4½" (2.5 cm x 11.6 cm)

2 N pieces, each 1" x 5½" (2.5 cm x 14.2 cm)

From the third Fabric 1 strip, cut the following pieces:
2 S pieces, each 1" x 9½" (2.5 cm x 24.6 cm)

From the first Fabric 2 strip, cut the following pieces:
11 U pieces, each 1" x 1½" (2.5 cm x 3.8 cm)
8 V pieces, each 1" x 2½" (2.5 cm x 6.4 cm)

From the second Fabric 2 strip, cut the following pieces:
5 V pieces, each 1" x 2½" (2.5 cm x 6.4 cm)
2 W pieces, each 1" x 3½" (2.5 cm x 9 cm)

5 Following the diagram and using the pieces cut in step 4, piece together horizontal strips 2–12. Sew the pieces end-to-end, with right sides together and using a ¼" (6 mm) seam allowance for all seams. Press all seams open.

6 Following the diagram, sew strip 1 (an S piece) to pieced strip 2. Then sew on the remaining pieced strips (strips 3–12), and lastly strip 13 (an S piece). Press all seams open. The completed "M" block should measure 7" x 9½" (18.1 cm x 24.6 cm).

CUT AND PIECE LETTER BLOCK "A"

7 To make letter block "A," you will need four of the 1" (2.5 cm) x WOF strips of Fabric 1 and two of the 1" (2.5 cm) x WOF strips of Fabric 2. From the first Fabric 1 strip, cut the following pieces:

2 D pieces, each 1" x 1" (2.5 cm x 2.5 cm)
3 E pieces, each 1" x 1½" (2.5 cm x 3.8 cm)
2 F pieces, each 1" x 2" (2.5 cm x 5.1 cm)
3 G pieces, each 1" x 2½" (2.5 cm x 6.4 cm)

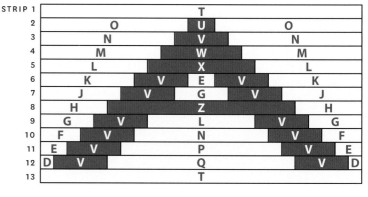

5 *Constructing letter block "M."*

8 *Constructing letter block "A."*

2 H pieces, each 1" x 3" (2.5 cm x 7.7 cm)

2 J pieces, each 1" x 3½" (2.5 cm x 9 cm)

2 K pieces, each 1" x 4" (2.5 cm x 10.3 cm)

From the second Fabric 1 strip, cut the following pieces:

3 L pieces, each 1" x 4½" (2.5 cm x 11.6 cm)

2 M pieces, each 1" x 5" (2.5 cm x 12.9 cm)

3 N pieces, each 1" x 5½" (2.5 cm x 14.2 cm)

From the third Fabric 1 strip, cut the following pieces:

2 O pieces, each 1" x 6" (2.5 cm x 15.5 cm)

1 P piece, 1" x 6½" (2.5 cm x 16.8 cm)

1 Q piece, 1" x 7½" (2.5 cm x 19.4 cm)

From the fourth Fabric 1 strip, cut the following pieces:

2 T pieces, each 1" x 12½" (2.5 cm x 32.4 cm)

From the first Fabric 2 strip, cut the following pieces:

1 U piece, 1" x 1½" (2.5 cm x 3.8 cm)

13 V pieces, each 1" x 2½" (2.5 cm x 6.4 cm)

1 W piece, 1" x 3½" (2.5 cm x 9 cm)

From the second Fabric 2 strip, cut the following pieces:

1 X piece, 1" x 4½" (2.5 cm x 11.6 cm)

1 Z piece, 1" x 7½" (2.5 cm x 19.4 cm)

8 Following the diagram and using the pieces cut in step 7, piece together horizontal strips 2–12. Press all seams open.

9 Following the diagram, sew strip 1 (a T piece) to pieced strip 2. Then sew on the remaining pieced strips (strips 3–12), and lastly strip 13 (a T piece). Press all seams open. The completed "A" block should measure 7" x 12½" (18.1 cm x 32.4 cm).

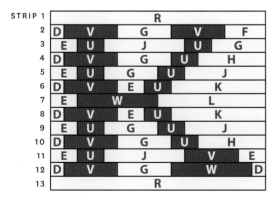

11 Constructing letter block "K."

CUT AND PIECE LETTER BLOCK "K"

10 To make letter block "K," you will need three of the 1" (2.5 cm) x WOF strips of Fabric 1 and two of the 1" (2.5 cm) x WOF strips of Fabric 2. From the first Fabric 1 strip, cut the following pieces:

7 D pieces, each 1" x 1" (2.5 cm x 2.5 cm)

8 E pieces, each 1" x 1½" (2.5 cm x 3.8 cm)

1 F piece, 1" x 2" (2.5 cm x 5.1 cm)

7 G pieces, each 1" x 2½" (2.5 cm x 6.4 cm)

From the second Fabric 1 strip, cut the following pieces:

2 H pieces, each 1" x 3" (2.5 cm x 7.7 cm)

4 J pieces, each 1" x 3½" (2.5 cm x 9 cm)

2 K pieces, each 1" x 4" (2.5 cm x 10.3 cm)

1 L piece, 1" x 4½" (2.5 cm x 11.6 cm)

From the third Fabric 1 strip, cut the following pieces:

2 R pieces, each 1" x 8½" (2.5 cm x 22 cm)

From the first Fabric 2 strip, cut the following pieces:

11 U pieces, each 1" x 1½" (2.5 cm x 3.8 cm)

8 V pieces, each 1" x 2½" (2.5 cm x 6.4 cm)

From the second Fabric 2 strip, cut the following pieces:

2 W pieces, each 1" x 3½" (2.5 cm x 9 cm)

11 Following the diagram and using the pieces cut in step 10, piece together horizontal strips 2–12. Press all seams open.

12 Following the diagram, sew strip 1 (an R piece) to pieced strip 2. Then sew on the remaining pieced strips (strips 3–12), and lastly strip 13 (an R piece). Press all seams open. The completed "K" block should measure 7" x 8½" (18.1 cm x 22 cm).

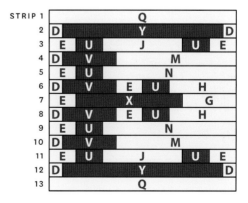

14 Constructing letter block "E."

CUT AND PIECE LETTER BLOCK "E"

13 To make letter block "E," you will need two of the 1" (2.5 cm) x WOF strips of Fabric 1 and one of the 1" (2.5 cm) x WOF strip of Fabric 2. From the first Fabric 1 strip, cut the following pieces:

8 D pieces, each 1" x 1" (2.5 cm x 2.5 cm)
9 E pieces, each 1" x 1½" (2.5 cm x 3.8 cm)
1 G piece, 1" x 2½" (2.5 cm x 6.4 cm)
2 H pieces, each 1" x 3" (2.5 cm x 7.7 cm)
2 J pieces, each 1" x 3½" (2.5 cm x 9 cm)

From the second Fabric 1 strip, cut the following pieces:
2 M pieces, each 1" x 5" (2.5 cm x 12.9 cm)
2 N pieces, each 1" x 5½" (2.5 cm x 14.2 cm)
2 Q pieces, each 1" x 7½" (2.5 cm x 19.4 cm)

From the Fabric 2 strip, cut the following pieces:
8 U pieces, each 1" x 1½" (2.5 cm x 3.8 cm)
4 V pieces, each 1" x 2½" (2.5 cm x 6.4 cm)
1 X piece, 1" x 4½" (2.5 cm x 11.6 cm)
2 Y pieces, each 1" x 6½" (2.5 cm x 16.8 cm)

14 Following the diagram and using the pieces cut in step 13, piece together horizontal strips 2–12. Press all seams open.

15 Following the diagram, sew the strips together as for the other letters. Press all seams open. The completed "E" block should measure 7" x 7½" (18.1 cm x 19.4 cm).

CONSTRUCT THE QUILT TOP

16 Following the diagram, sew the four letter blocks together and press the seams open. Add on a B piece at each end of the letter blocks and press the seams to the side toward the B pieces.

17 Sew the A piece to the top of the letter block section, following the diagram. Press the seam to the side toward the A piece. Then sew the C piece to the bottom of the letter block section. Press the seam to the side toward the C piece.

CUT AND PIECE THE QUILT BACK

18 To make the quilt back, cut two 58" (150 cm) x WOF pieces out of the backing fabric. Trim the selvages off of each of the pieces. Sew the pieces right sides together, along one long edge, and press the seam allowance to the side.

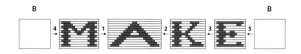

16 *Sewing together the letter block section.*

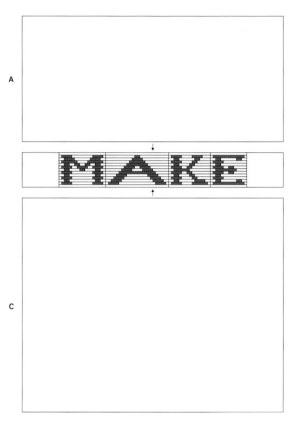

17 *Completing the quilt top.*

FINISH THE QUILT

19 Layer the quilt top, batting, and quilt back to make a quilt sandwich (page 29). Baste together with quilting pins or basting stitches (page 30).

20 Quilt as desired (page 31). After quilting, trim off the excess batting and backing fabric to align them with the edges of the quilt top, and square up all sides of the quilt if necessary.

21 From the binding fabric, cut seven 2½" (6 cm) x WOF strips. Cut off the selvages and sew the seven strips together end-to-end to create the continuous binding (page 31). Bind the quilt as desired (page 33).

central parkway

For this quilt, I drew inspiration from the Erich Kunzel Center for Arts and Education, a performance facility on the grounds of Cincinnati's School for Creative and Performing Arts. When I first saw the building, I was immediately drawn to its shimmering surface, but upon further study, I became captivated by the stair-stepping grid that surrounds each diamond shape.

As in many traditional quilt patterns, this design is made up of blocks. I used a total of nine, but you can make more or fewer to change the quilt's finished size. The overall design looks quite complex, however the blocks—each made from strips of fabric in just two colors—are simple to construct.

To show how different a quilt pattern can look when you use the same colors, but in reverse areas of the design, I used the same two fabrics in both versions—a solid dark purplish blue and a solid raspberry. Both colors are quite saturated, but the blue is darker in value than the raspberry. If you choose your own two colors, be sure to select ones that have enough contrast to make the graphic pattern stand out boldly.

The blue in the first version appears darker than in the second, because there is so much more of it in the quilt overall. This is an example of color influence, or color relativity: The way we perceive a color depends on what surrounds it. Similarly, the raspberry appears richer and more vibrant in the second version because the color is so pronounced there.

FINISHED QUILT SIZE
60½" x 60½" (151 cm x 151 cm)

FABRICS
The fabric amounts are based on using 44–45" (112–115 cm) wide fabrics.

COLORWAY 1
RED GRID ON BLUE GROUND

FABRIC 1: 2¾ yards (2.6 m) of a solid dark blue, such as Clothworks *American Made Brand Cotton Solids* in Dark Indigo (96)

FABRIC 2: 1½ yards (1.4 m) of a solid raspberry, such as Clothworks *American Made Brand Cotton Solids* in Dark Raspberry (75)

BACKING FABRIC: 4 yards (3.7 m) of a solid purple, such as Clothworks *American Made Brand Cotton Solids* in Purple (27)

BINDING FABRIC: ½ yard (50 cm) more of Fabric 1

COLORWAY 2
BLUE GRID ON RED GROUND

FABRIC 1: 2¾ yards (2.6 m) of a solid raspberry, such as Clothworks *American Made Brand Cotton Solids* in Dark Raspberry (75)

FABRIC 2: 1½ yards (1.4 m) of a solid dark blue, such as Clothworks *American Made Brand Cotton Solids* in Dark Indigo (96)

BACKING FABRIC: 4 yards (3.7 m) of a solid purple, such as Clothworks *American Made Brand Cotton Solids* in Purple (27)

BINDING FABRIC: ½ yard (50 cm) more of Fabric 1

OTHER MATERIALS
+ 65" x 65" (161 cm x 161 cm) piece of batting (or a twin-sized package)
+ All-purpose thread for piecing
+ Dark blue quilting thread for colorway 1, OR raspberry for colorway 2

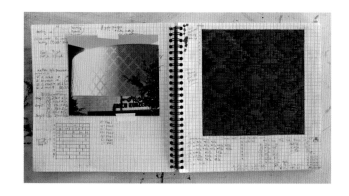

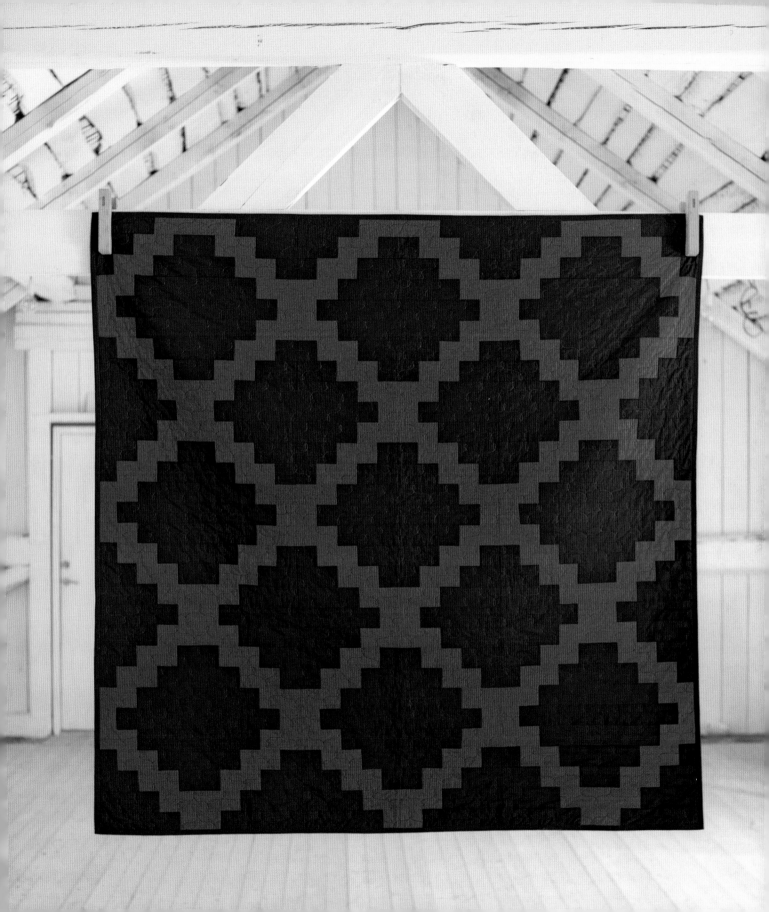

CUT THE QUILT-TOP PIECES

1 From Fabric 1—using a rotary cutter, straight edge, and a cutting mat—cut width of fabric (WOF) strips (for making the WOF pieced sections) as follows:

Two 2½" (6.2 cm) x WOF strips
Three 4½" (11.2 cm) x WOF strips
Two 6½" (16.2 cm) x WOF strips
Three 8½" (21.2 cm) x WOF strips
One 12½" (31.2 cm) x WOF strip
One 16½" (41.2 cm) x WOF strip

2 From Fabric 1, cut three more 2½" (6.2 cm) x WOF strips (for making the individually pieced rows). Label your pieces as you cut them.

From the first Fabric 1 strip, cut the following pieces:
4 G pieces, each 2½" x 2½" (6.2 cm x 6.2 cm)
6 H pieces, each 2½" x 4½" (6.2 cm x 11.2 cm)

From the second Fabric 1 strip, cut the following pieces:
4 J pieces, each 2½" x 6½" (6.2 cm x 16.2 cm)
1 K piece, 2½" x 8½" (6.2 cm x 21.2 cm)

From the third Fabric 1 strip, cut the following pieces:
1 K piece, 2½" x 8½" (6.2 cm x 21.2 cm)
2 L pieces, each 2½" x 12½" (6.2 cm x 31.2 cm)

3 From Fabric 2, cut Width of Fabric (WOF) strips (for making the WOF pieced sections) as follows:

Two 2½" (6.2 cm) x WOF strips
Seven 4½" (11.2 cm) x WOF strips
One 8½" (21.2 cm) x WOF strip

4 From Fabric 2, cut two more 2½" (6.2 cm) x WOF strips (for making the individually pieced rows). Label your pieces as you cut them.

From the first Fabric 2 strip, cut the following pieces:
8 M pieces, each 2½" x 4½" (6.2 cm x 11.2 cm)

From the second Fabric 2 strip, cut the following pieces:
4 M pieces, each 2½" x 4½" (6.2 cm x 11.2 cm)
2 N pieces, each 2½" x 8½" (6.2 cm x 21.2 cm)

CONSTRUCT THE A ROWS

5 Using two 6½" (16.2 cm) x WOF strips of Fabric 1 and one 8½" (21.2 cm) x WOF strip of Fabric 2, make the pieced section for the A rows. Following the diagram, sew one Fabric 1 strip to the Fabric 2 strip along one long edge, with right sides together and using a ¼" (6 mm) seam allowance for all seams. Then sew the other Fabric 1 strip to the opposite side of the Fabric 2 strip to complete the pieced section for the A rows. Press the seams to the side, toward the darker fabric. From this pieced section, subcut 16 A rows each 2½" (6.2 cm) wide. Pin labels to your rows as you cut them.

6 To make all nine blocks of the quilt top, you need two more A rows. Using the individual strips cut in steps 2 and 4, construct these A rows singly, using two J pieces (Fabric 1) and one N piece (Fabric 2) for each row. Following the diagram, sew one J piece to the N piece, then sew on the other J piece to complete one A row. Make a second A row in the same way. You now have a total of 18 A rows—two for each of the nine blocks.

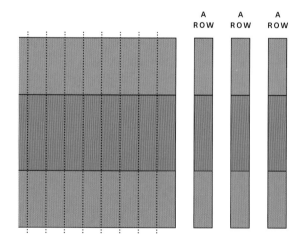

5 *Cutting 16 A rows from the pieced section.*

6 *Piecing single A rows.*

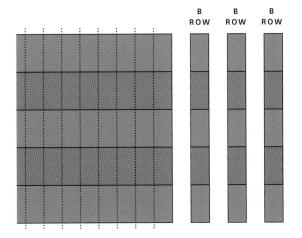

7 *Cutting 16 B rows from the pieced section.*

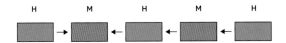

8 *Piecing single B rows.*

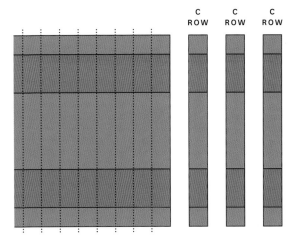

9 *Cutting 16 C rows from the pieced section.*

10 *Piecing single C rows.*

CONSTRUCT THE B ROWS

7 Using three 4½" (11.2 cm) x WOF strips of Fabric 1 and two 4½" (11.2 cm) x WOF strips of Fabric 2, make the pieced section for the B rows. Following the diagram, sew one Fabric 1 strip to one Fabric 2 strip along one long edge. Then sew on one Fabric 1 strip, the remaining Fabric 2 strip, and the remaining Fabric 1 strip. Press all seams to the side, toward the darker fabric. From this pieced section, subcut 16 B rows each 2½" (6.2 cm) wide. Label your rows as you cut them.

8 To make all nine blocks of the quilt top, you need two more B rows. Using the individual strips cut in steps 2 and 4, construct these B rows singly, using three H pieces (Fabric 1) and two M pieces (Fabric 2) for each row. Following the diagram, sew one H piece to one M piece. Then sew on another H piece, the remaining M piece, and the remaining H piece to complete one B row. Make a second B row in the same way. You now have a total of 18 B rows—two for each of the nine blocks.

CONSTRUCT THE C ROWS

9 Using two 2½" (6.2 cm) x WOF strips of Fabric 1, one 8½" (21.2 cm) x WOF strip of Fabric 1, and two 4½" (11.2 cm) x WOF strips of Fabric 2, make the pieced section for the C rows. Following the diagram, sew one 2½" (6.2 cm) Fabric 1 strip to one of the Fabric 2 strips along one long edge. Then sew on the 8½" (21.2 cm) Fabric 1 strip, the remaining Fabric 2 strip, and the remaining Fabric 1 strip to complete the pieced section for the C rows. Press all seams to the side, toward the darker fabric. From this pieced section, subcut 16 C rows each 2½" (6.2 cm) wide. Pin labels to your rows as you cut them.

10 To make all nine blocks of the quilt top, you need two more C rows. Using the individual strips cut in steps 2 and 4, construct these C rows singly, using two G pieces (Fabric 1), one K piece (Fabric 1), and two M pieces (Fabric 2) for each row. Following the diagram, sew one G piece to one M piece. Then sew on the K piece, the remaining M piece, and the remaining G piece to complete one C row. Make a second C row in the same way. You now have a total of 18 C rows—two for each of the nine blocks.

CONSTRUCT THE D ROWS

11 Using one 12½" (31.2 cm) x WOF strip of Fabric 1 and two 4½" (11.2 cm) x WOF strips of Fabric 2, make the pieced section for the D rows. Following the diagram, sew one Fabric 2 strip to the Fabric 1 strip along one long edge. Then sew the other Fabric 2 strip to the opposite side of the Fabric 1 strip to complete the pieced section for the D rows. Press all seams to the side, toward the darker fabric. From this pieced section, subcut 16 D rows each 2½" (6.2 cm) wide. Label your rows as you cut them.

12 To make all nine blocks of the quilt top, you need two more D rows. Using the individual strips cut in steps 2 and 4, construct these D rows singly, using one L piece (Fabric 1) and two M pieces (Fabric 2) for each row. Following the diagram, sew one M piece to the L piece, then sew on the other M piece to complete one D row. Make a second D row in the same way. You now have a total of 18 D rows—two for each of the nine blocks.

CONSTRUCT THE E ROWS

13 Using one 16½" (41.2 cm) x WOF strip of Fabric 1 and two 2½" (6.2 cm) x WOF strips of Fabric 2, make the pieced section for the E rows. Following the diagram, sew one Fabric 2 strip to the Fabric 1 strip along one long edge. Then sew the other Fabric 2 strip to the opposite side of the Fabric 1 strip to complete the pieced section for the E rows. Press all seams to the side, toward the darker fabric. From this pieced section, subcut nine E rows each 2½" (6.2 cm) wide. Label your rows as you cut them. There is one E row in each of the nine blocks.

CONSTRUCT THE F ROWS

14 Using two 8½" (21.2 cm) x WOF strips of Fabric 1 and one 4½" (11.2 cm) x WOF strip of Fabric 2, make the pieced section for the F rows. Following the diagram, sew one Fabric 1 strip to the Fabric 2 strip along one long edge. Then sew the other Fabric 1 strip to the opposite side of the Fabric 2 strip to complete the pieced section for the F rows. Press all seams to the side, toward the darker fabric. From this pieced section, subcut nine F rows each 2½" (6.2 cm) wide. Label your rows as you cut them. There is one F row in each of the nine blocks.

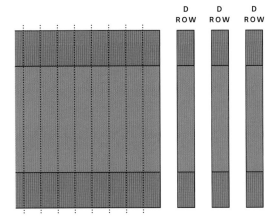

11 *Cutting 16 D rows from the pieced section.*

12 *Piecing single D rows.*

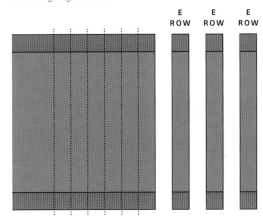

13 *Cutting nine E rows from the pieced section.*

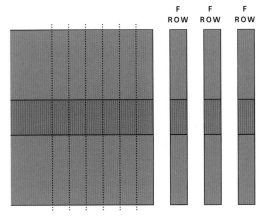

14 *Cutting nine F rows from the pieced section.*

CONSTRUCT THE QUILT BLOCKS

15 Each quilt block is made up of two A rows, two C rows, two D rows, one E row, and one F row. Following the diagram, sew one A row to one B row. Then add on one C row, one D row, one E row, the second D row, the second C row, the second B row, the second A row, and the F row to complete one block. Press all seams open. The finished block should measure 20½" x 20½" (51.2 cm x 51.2 cm).

16 Repeat step 15 eight more times to make a total of nine blocks.

CONSTRUCT THE QUILT TOP

17 Sew the blocks together in three rows of three blocks each.

18 Sew the rows together to complete the quilt top.

CUT AND PIECE THE QUILT BACK

19 To make the quilt back, cut two 68" (173 cm) x WOF pieces out of the backing fabric. Trimming off the selvages as you do so, trim each of the pieces *lengthwise* so that they measure 34½" x 68" (88 cm x 173cm). Sew the pieces right sides together, along one long edge, and press the seam to the side.

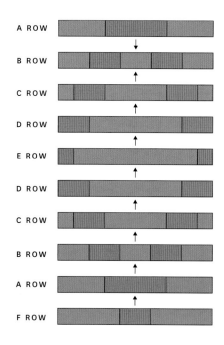

15 *Making the block.*

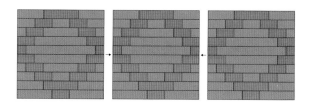

17 *Sewing the blocks together in rows.*

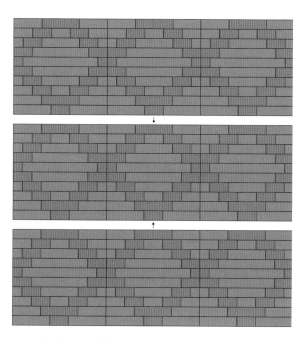

18 *Sewing the rows of blocks together.*

FINISH THE QUILT

20 Layer the quilt top, batting, and quilt back to make a quilt sandwich (page 29). Baste together with quilting pins or basting stitches (page 30).

21 Quilt as desired (page 31). After quilting, trim off the excess batting and backing fabric to align them with the edges of the quilt top, and square up all sides of the quilt if necessary.

22 From the binding fabric, cut seven 2½" (6 cm) x WOF strips. Cut off the selvages and sew the seven strips together end-to-end to create the continuous binding (page 31). Bind the quilt as desired (page 33).

columbus

My Columbus project, a small wall hanging or table runner, was inspired by two large water towers outside Columbus, Ohio. My husband and I were driving past them one day and I was immediately captivated by the colors that they were painted—a creamy white and a light blue—and even more so by the fact that they were each painted with stripes in various widths. I loved how the two water towers looked next to each other and how the width of the stripes created a great horizontal linear pattern, so that is what I played with for my design. Rather than create color palettes based on the actual colors of the water towers, which are colors that I work with quite often, I decided to create two completely different palettes.

I feature a solid light lime green and a solid dark gray in the first color palette. The overall color temperature of this palette is cool, as both the green and the gray are cool colors. The gray acts as a neutral, and I used it for the binding of the quilt as well, which helps to frame the design. The gray also draws more attention to the green sections of the quilt, since it causes a visual shift where the two colors touch. I like the contrast of the lighter value green with the darker value gray, and the combination of two strongly contrasting colors creates a lot of movement throughout the quilt pattern.

The warmer color palette of the second version consists of a solid warm cream combined with a warm mottled red. This red is not as visually flat as true solid because of the slight variations in color throughout the fabric. In this version the neutral is the cream, although I placed it in the areas that were made of the lime in the first version. By making this change, different areas of the quilt are highlighted: your eye is drawn to the red, rather than the cream. I used the cream for the binding so that the red sections would be nicely framed.

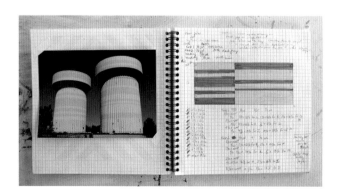

FINISHED QUILT SIZE
30½" x 12½" (77 cm x 31 cm)

FABRICS
The fabric amounts are based on using 44–45" (112–115 cm) wide fabrics.

COLORWAY 1
LIME AND GRAY

FABRIC 1: ⅓ yard (35 cm) of a solid lime, such as Clothworks *American Made Brand Cotton Solids* in Lime (18)

FABRIC 2: ⅓ yard (35 cm) of a solid dark gray, such as Clothworks *American Made Brand Cotton Solids* in Dark Gray (07)

BACKING FABRIC: ⅝ yard (60 cm) more of Fabric 2

BINDING FABRIC: ¼ yard (25 cm) more of Fabric 2

COLORWAY 2
BEIGE AND RED

FABRIC 1: ⅓ yard (35 cm) of a solid light beige, such as Robert Kaufman *Kona Cotton Solids* in Sand (1323)

FABRIC 2: ⅓ yard (35 cm) of a solid dark red, such as Moda *Rouenneries* by French General in Rouge

BACKING FABRIC: ⅝ yard (60 cm) more of Fabric 1

BINDING FABRIC: ¼ yard (25 cm) more of Fabric 1

OTHER MATERIALS
+ 33" x 15" (84 cm x 38 cm) piece of batting
+ All-purpose thread for piecing
+ Light gray quilting thread for colorway 1, OR off-white for colorway 2

CUT THE QUILT TOP PIECES

1 Using a rotary cutter, straight edge, and a cutting mat, cut one 1½" (3.7 cm) x width of fabric (WOF) strip from Fabric 1, cutting from selvage to selvage. Subcut this strip into three strips each 1½" x 12½" (3.7 cm x 31.2 cm) for one C piece, one E piece, and one G piece. Pin labels to your pieces as you cut them.

2 From Fabric 1, cut one 2½" (6.2 cm) x WOF strip. Subcut this strip into one 2½" x 12½" (6.2 cm x 31.2 cm) strip for one A piece and one 2" x 18½" (5 cm x 31.2 cm) strip for one M piece, trimming the width of the strip to 2" (5 cm) when cutting the M piece.

3 From Fabric 1, cut one 4½" (11.2 cm) x WOF strip. Subcut this strip into one 4½" x 18½" (11.2 cm x 47.2 cm) strip for one O piece and one 3½" x 18½" (8.7 cm x 47.2 cm) strip for one K piece, trimming the width of the strip to 3½" (8.7 cm) when cutting the K piece.

4 From Fabric 2, cut two 1½" (3.7 cm) x WOF strips. Subcut the first of these strips into two strips each 1½" x 12½" (3.7 cm x 31.2 cm) strip for one B piece and one F piece. Subcut the second strip into one 1½" x 18½" (3.7 cm x 47.2 cm) strip for one L piece and one 1" x 18½" (2.4 cm x 47.2 cm) strip for one N piece, trimming the width of the strip to 1" (2.4 cm) when cutting the N piece.

5 From Fabric 2, cut one 2½" (6.2 cm) x WOF strip. Subcut this strip into one 2½" x 12½" (6.2 cm x 31.2 cm) strip for one H piece and one 2½" x 18½" (6.2 cm x 47.2 cm) strip for one J piece.

6 From Fabric 2, cut one 3½" (8.7 cm) x WOF strip. Trim this strip to 3½" x 12½" (8.7 cm x 31.2 cm) for one D piece.

CONSTRUCT THE PIECED SECTIONS

7 Use the A, B, C, D, E, F, G, and H pieces for pieced section 1. Following the diagram, sew the A piece to the B piece, with right sides together and using a ¼" (6 mm) seam allowance for all seams. Then sew on the C, D, E, F, G, and H pieces as shown to complete section 1. Press all seams to the side.

8 Use the J, K, L, M, N, and O pieces for section 2. Following the diagram, sew the J piece to the K piece. Then sew on the L, M, N, and O pieces as shown to complete section 2. Press all seams to the side.

CONSTRUCT THE QUILT TOP

9 Following the diagram, sew pieced section 1 to the pieced section 2. Press the seam open.

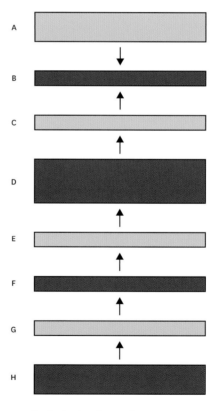

7   *Sewing together section 1.*

CUT THE QUILT BACK

10 To make the quilt back, cut one 20" (51 cm) x WOF piece out of the backing fabric. Trimming off the selvages as you do so, trim the piece *lengthwise* so that it measures 20" x 38" (51 cm x 97 cm) for the backing.

FINISH THE QUILT

11 Layer the quilt top, batting, and quilt back to make a quilt sandwich (page 29). Baste together with quilting pins or basting stitches (page 30).

12 Quilt as desired (page 31). After quilting, trim off the excess batting and backing fabric to align them with the edges of the quilt top, and square up all sides of the quilt if necessary.

13 From the binding fabric, cut three 2½" (6 cm) x WOF strips. Cut off the selvages and sew the three strips together end-to-end to create the continuous binding (page 31). Bind the quilt as desired (page 33).

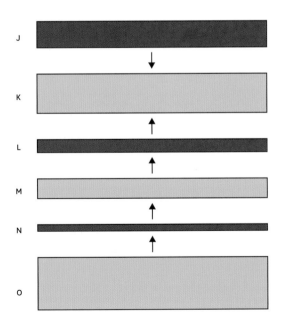

8 *Sewing together section 2.*

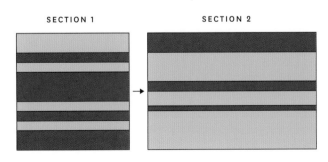

9 *Completing the quilt top.*

indian hill

The wooden dock at a family friend's pond was my starting point for this quilt. I've been on this dock many times throughout my life, but it wasn't until recently that I noticed how the wood interlocks in an intricate herringbone pattern.

Six solid cotton colors form the palette for the first version of the quilt—shades of orange, red, berry, periwinkle, indigo, and light khaki. If you're familiar with my work, you may recognize that this is a lot of color for me. To create order in what otherwise might have felt too discordant for my taste, I arranged the colors with great care in two distinct warm and cool groups. This creates a crisp woven effect. I like the way the warm and cool colors look as if they're bouncing off one another.

The second color palette is made up of a combination of prints and solid cottons in shades of green, black, light gray, and pale beige. Instead of creating two distinct groupings of fabrics, I made sure that each grouping of fabrics in this version contained at least one green fabric and one gray fabric. The design still suggests quite a lot of movement but is more harmonious than the first version.

FINISHED QUILT SIZE
51½" x 51½" (129 cm x 129 cm)

FABRICS
The fabric amounts are based on using 44–45" (112–115 cm) wide fabrics.

COLORWAY 1
ORANGE, REDS, BLUES, AND PALE BEIGE

FABRIC 1: ⅝ yard (60 cm) of a solid pale beige, such as Clothworks *American Made Brand Cotton Solids* in Light Khaki (11)

FABRIC 2: ⅝ yard (60 cm) of a solid light blue, such as Clothworks *American Made Brand Cotton Solids* in Perwinkle (85)

FABRIC 3: ⅝ yard (60 cm) of a solid dark blue, such as Clothworks *American Made Brand Cotton Solids* in Dark Indigo (96)

FABRIC 4: ¾ yard (70 cm) of a solid orange, such as Clothworks *American Made Brand Cotton Solids* in Dark Orange (37)

FABRIC 5: ¾ yard (70 cm) of a solid raspberry, such as Clothworks *American Made Brand Cotton Solids* in Dark Raspberry (75)

FABRIC 6: ¾ yard (70 cm) of a solid dark fuchsia, such as Clothworks *American Made Brand Cotton Solids* in Dark Fuchsia (78)

BACKING FABRIC: 3½ yards (3.2 m) more of Fabric 1

BINDING FABRIC: ½ yard (50 cm) more of Fabric 1

COLORWAY 2
GREENS, BLACK, LIGHT GRAY, AND PALE BEIGE

FABRIC 1: ⅝ yard (60 cm) of a solid light gray, such as Robert Kaufman *Kona Cotton Solids* in Ash (1007)

FABRIC 2: ⅝ yard (60 cm) of a solid lime, such as FreeSpirit *Designer Solids* in Citrine (S86)

FABRIC 3: ⅝ yard (60 cm) of a fine white stripe on a black ground, such as FreeSpirit *Ansonia – Fine Stripe* by Denyse Schmidt in Onyx

FABRIC 4: ¾ yard (70 cm) of a solid pale beige, such as Clothworks *American Made Brand Cotton Solids* in Light Khaki (11)

FABRIC 5: ¾ yard (70 cm) of a lime print, such as FreeSpirit *Ansonia – Medallion* by Denyse Schmidt in Mossy

FABRIC 6: ¾ yard (70 cm) of a lime and black print, such as FreeSpirit *Ansonia – Stitch* by Denyse Schmidt in Mossy

BACKING FABRIC: 3½ yards (3.2 m) more of Fabric 4

BINDING FABRIC: ½ yard (50 cm) more of Fabric 3

OTHER MATERIALS
+ 56" x 56" (140 cm x 140 cm) piece of batting (or a twin-sized package)
+ All-purpose thread for piecing
+ Water-soluble marking pen or pencil
+ Off-white quilting thread for both colorways

CUT THE QUILT-TOP PIECES

1 Using a rotary cutter, straight edge, and a cutting mat, cut four 4½" (11.2 cm) x width of fabric (WOF) pieces from Fabric 1, cutting from selvage to selvage.

2 From Fabric 2, cut four 4½" (11.2 cm) x WOF strips.

3 From Fabric 3, cut four 4½" (11.2 cm) x WOF strips.

4 From Fabric 4, cut five 4½" (11.2 cm) x WOF strips.

5 From Fabric 5, cut five 4½" (11.2 cm) x WOF strips.

6 From Fabric 6, cut five 4½" (11.2 cm) x WOF strips.

CONSTRUCT THE A BLOCKS

7 Sew one 4½" (11.2 cm) x WOF strip of Fabric 1 to one 4½" (11.2 cm) x WOF strip of Fabric 2 along one long edge, with right sides together and using a ¼" (6 mm) seam allowance for all seams. Sew one 4½" (11.2 cm) x WOF strip of Fabric 3 to the opposite side of the Fabric 2 strip to complete one pieced section for the A blocks. Press the seams to the side, toward the darker fabric. Repeat this step three more times to make a total of four 12½" (31.2 cm) wide pieced sections for the A blocks.

8 Cut three 12½" x 12½" (31.2 cm x 31.2 cm) A blocks from each of three of the pieced sections made in step 7. Cut one 12½" x 12½" (31.2 cm x 31.2 cm) A block from the remaining pieced section, for a total of 10 A blocks.

CONSTRUCT THE B BLOCKS

9 Sew one 4½" (11.2 cm) x WOF strip of Fabric 4 to one 4½" (11.2 cm) x WOF strip of Fabric 5 along one long edge. Sew one 4½" (11.2 cm) x WOF strip of Fabric 6 to the opposite side of the Fabric 5 strip to complete one pieced section for the B blocks. Press the seams to the side, toward the darker fabric. Repeat this step four more times to make a total of five 12½" (31.2 cm) wide pieced sections for the B blocks.

10 Cut three 12½" x 12½" (31.2 cm x 31.2 cm) B blocks from each of four of the pieced sections made in step 9. Cut two 12½" x 12½" (31.2 cm x 31.2 cm) B blocks from the remaining pieced section, for a total of 14 B blocks.

CONSTRUCT THE QUILT TOP

NOTE: The quilt is constructed by setting the blocks on point. To do this, you first sew the blocks together in horizontal rows that are made up of differing numbers of blocks. While the rows are constructed, the strips on all A blocks are horizontal and the strips on all B blocks are vertical. Once the rows are all sewn together, the excess triangles along the edges are trimmed off.

11 Following the diagram for step 17 on page 150, construct row 1. Sew one B block to one A block. Press the seam to the side, toward the right.

12 Following the diagram, construct row 2. Sew one A block to one B block. Then add on one more B block and another A block. Press the seams to the side, toward the left.

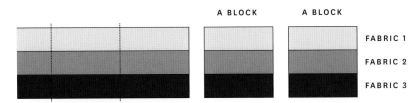

8   *Cutting the A blocks from the pieced strips of Fabrics 1, 2, and 3.*

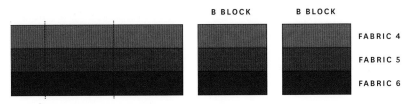

10   *Cutting the B blocks from the pieced strips of Fabrics 4, 5, and 6.*

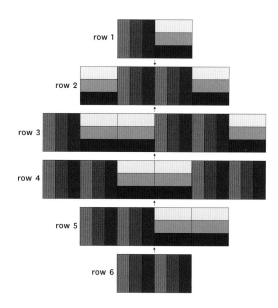

row 1

row 2

row 3

row 4

row 5

row 6

17 *Sewing together the rows.*

18 *Trimming the finished quilt top.*

13 Following the diagram, construct row 3. Sew one B block to one A block. Then add on one more A block, two B blocks, and another A block to complete the row. Press the seams to the side, toward the right.

14 Following the diagram, construct row 4. Sew one B block to another B block. Then add on two A blocks, followed by two B blocks to complete the row. Press the seams to the side, toward the left.

15 Following the diagram, construct row 5. Sew one B block to another B block. Then add on two A blocks to complete the row. Press the seams to the side, toward the right.

16 To construct row 6, sew the last two B blocks together. Press the seam to the side, toward the left.

17 Following the diagram, sew rows 1–6 together, making sure to nestle the seams of each block between the rows. Press all seams to the side.

18 Using the water-soluble marker pen and a straight edge, draw a line along the perimeter of the quilt top as shown in the diagram, in order to mark straight side edges. Use the drawn line as a cutting line and trim off the excess fabric with a rotary cutter and straight edge to square up the quilt top.

CUT AND PIECE THE QUILT BACK

19 To make the quilt back, cut two 59" (150 cm) x WOF pieces out of the backing fabric. Trimming off the selvages as you do so, trim each of the pieces *lengthwise* so that they measure 30" x 59" (78 cm x 150 cm). Sew the pieces right sides together, along one long edge, and press the seam to the side.

FINISH THE QUILT

20 Layer the quilt top, batting, and quilt back to make a quilt sandwich (page 29). Baste together with quilting pins or basting stitches (page 30).

21 Quilt as desired (page 31). After quilting, trim off the excess batting and backing fabric to align them with the edges of the quilt top, and square up all sides of the quilt if necessary.

22 From the binding fabric, cut six 2½" (6 cm) x WOF strips. Cut off the selvages and sew the six strips together end-to-end to create the continuous binding (page 31). Bind the quilt as desired (page 33).

homage

This design is inspired by the work of Josef Albers, in particular his *Homage to the Square* series of paintings that explored how colors work with each other and react against each other. Rather than duplicate Albers's work in which the squares are nestled within each other, I have changed my version so that the three squares are on the same plane, that is, they all rest on the same ground line. This pillow cover is easy to construct and has a strong visual impact. An envelope closure on the back of the cover makes it easy to insert your pillow form and remove it when you need to clean the cover.

For my first version of the design, I created an analogous color palette using three shades of yellow, surrounded by white sashing around the block. I placed the lightest fabric in the center and ringed it with two darker yellows: a mid-tone butter yellow and a darker saffron yellow.

You'll find nine other versions of the Homage design on page 15. They illustrate different types of color palettes: monochromatic, complementary, cool, warm, neutral, analogous, secondary, muted, and saturated. Making this cover in your own color scheme is a great way to experiment with colors and patterns.

FINISHED COVER SIZE

19½" x 19½" (49 cm x 49 cm)

FABRICS

The fabric amounts are based on using 44–45" (112–115 cm) wide fabrics.

FABRIC 1: ¼ yard (25 cm), OR a 9" (23 cm) square, of a solid light yellow, such as Clothworks *American Made Brand Cotton Solids* in Light Yellow (08)

FABRIC 2: ¼ yard (25 cm) of a solid bright medium yellow, such as Clothworks *American Made Brand Cotton Solids* in Dark Yellow (10)

FABRIC 3: ¼ yard (25 cm) of a solid dark gold, such as Clothworks *American Made Brand Cotton Solids* in Dark Gold (69)

FABRIC 4: ¼ yard (25 cm) of a solid white, such as Clothworks *American Made Brand Cotton Solids* in White (01)

BACKING FABRIC FOR PILLOW-COVER FRONT: 26" (65 cm) square of white cotton fabric

FABRIC FOR PILLOW-COVER BACK: ½ yard (50 cm) more of Fabric 4

OTHER MATERIALS

+ 24" x 24" (60 cm x 60 cm) of batting

+ All-purpose thread for piecing and sewing cover together

+ White quilting thread

+ 20" x 20" (50 cm x 50 cm) premade pillow form

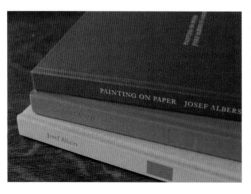

CUT THE PILLOW-COVER TOP PIECES

1   Using a rotary cutter, straight edge, and a cutting mat, cut one 6½" x 6½" (16.2 cm x 16.2 cm) square from Fabric 1 for one A piece. Label your pieces as you cut them.

2   Using a rotary cutter, straight edge, and a cutting mat, cut one 2½" (6.2 cm) x width of fabric (WOF) strip and one 4½" (11.2 cm) x WOF strip, from Fabric 2, cutting from selvage to selvage. Subcut the 2½" (6.2 cm) x WOF strip into two 2½" x 6½" (6.2 cm x 16.2 cm) strips for two B pieces. Trim the 4½" (11.2 cm) WOF strip to 4½" x 10½" (11.2 cm x 26.2 cm) for one C piece.

3   From Fabric 3, cut one 2½" (6.2 cm) x WOF and one 4½" (11.2 cm) x WOF strip. Subcut the 2½" (6.2 cm) x WOF strip into two 2½" x 10½" (6.2 cm x 26.2 cm) strips for two D pieces. Trim the 4½" (11.2 cm) WOF strip to 4½" x 14½" (11.2 cm x 36.2 cm) for one E piece.

4   From Fabric 4, cut two 3½" (8.7 cm) x WOF strips. Subcut the first strip into two 3½" x 14½" (8.7 cm x 36.2 cm) for two F pieces, and subcut the other strip into two 3½" x 20½" (8.7 cm x 51.2 cm) pieces for two G pieces.

CONSTRUCT THE PILLOW-COVER FRONT TOP

5   Following the diagram, sew one B piece to the right side of the A piece, with right sides together and using a ¼" (6 mm) seam allowance for all seams. Sew the other B piece to the left side of the A piece and press the seams to the side, toward the B pieces. Then sew the C piece to the top of the pieced section. Press the seam to the side, toward the C piece.

6   Following the diagram, sew one D piece to the right side of pieced section and the other D piece to the left side of the pieced section. Press the seams to the side, toward the D pieces. Then sew the E piece to the top of the pieced section. Press the seam to the side, toward the E piece.

7   Sew one F piece to the right side of the pieced section, and sew the other F piece to the left side of the pieced section, following the diagram. Press the seams to the side, toward the F pieces.

8   Following the diagram, sew one G piece to the top of the pieced section, and sew the other G piece to the bottom of the pieced section to complete the pillow-cover front top. Press the seams to the side, toward the G pieces.

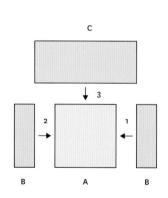

5   *Sewing together the A, B, and C pieces.*

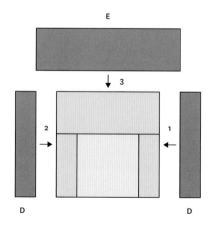

6   *Sewing on the D and E pieces.*

FINISH THE PILLOW-COVER FRONT

9   Layer the batting between the pillow-cover front top and the 26"
    (65 cm) square of backing fabric to make a quilt sandwich (page
    29). Baste together with quilting pins (page 30).

10 Quilt as desired (page 31). After quilting, trim off the excess
    batting and backing fabric to align them with the edges of the
    pillow-cover front top, and square up all sides of the quilted
    piece if necessary.

SEW ON THE PILLOW-COVER BACK

11 Make the pillow-cover back in two pieces to create an envelope
    opening. First, cut one 15½" (38.7 cm) x WOF strip from the
    pillow-cover back fabric. Subcut this strip into two 15½" x 20½"
    (38.7 cm x 51.2 cm) rectangles for the two back pieces.

12 Complete the pillow-cover back following steps 18–21 for the
    Covington Pillow Cover on page 122.

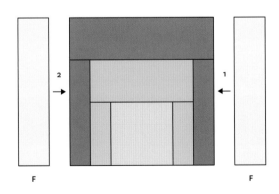

7   *Sewing on the F pieces.*

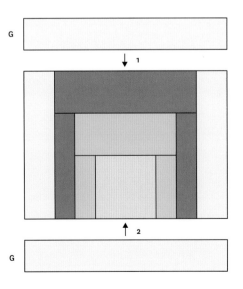

8   *Sewing on the G pieces to complete the front top.*

TEMPLATES

The templates for Union Terminal and Springfield quilts are shown here at 50% of their actual size. Enlarge as directed for correct sizes.

○ *center circle*

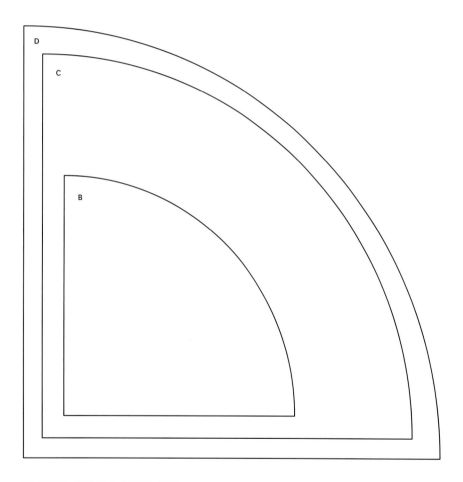

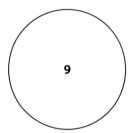

QUARTER CIRCLE TEMPLATES
For Union Terminal on page 124.
Enlarge 200%. Draw a full quarter
circle for each template.

CIRCLE TEMPLATES
For Springfield on page 50.
Enlarge 200%.

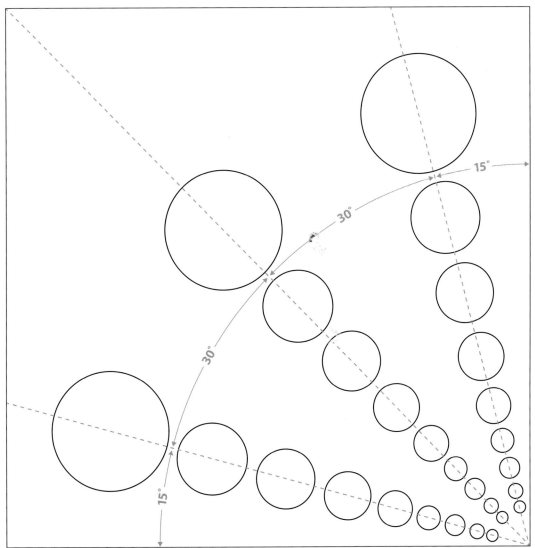

center of design

CIRCLE LAYOUT TEMPLATES
For Springfield on page 50. Enlarge 200%.

ACKNOWLEDGMENTS

This project would not have been possible without love, support, and guidance from the following people, all of whom I am lucky to have in my life:

To my mother, Jane, I owe my love of craft and handmade. Thank you for sharing your gifts of creativity, the desire to make things by hand, and for all of your support throughout the process of writing this book. To my father, Mike, thank you for your gift of loving to learn, and for always encouraging my creative adventures. Thank you also to Susan, Kate, Mitzi, and Terry.

Thanks must also go to my local quilting friends Kara Sanders and Sarah Smith for design consultations at coffee shops; to Gillian Krygowski, Sue Erhart, and Christine Doyle for their encouragement, and to Jill Montgomery for long-arm quilting advice. Thank you also to three other dear friends who I consider my sisters in craft: Amy Butler, for teaching me to always follow my heart and for helping me find the confidence to live the life I want—you fill the world with the most amazing color. Heather Givens, for always lending an ear, for holding my hand through the telephone line, and for exuberant cheerleading when I needed it. Denyse Schmidt, for the beautiful foreword to this book and for all of your encouragement throughout this project—you showed me the ropes and shared such insight, and for that I am grateful. Thank you also for continuing to inspire me and the rest of the world with your own incredible work.

Many thanks to my generous sponsors, Robert Kaufman, FreeSpirit Fabric, Clothworks, Coats, Aurifil, and Pellon, for providing materials for many of the projects. Your beautiful goods continue to inspire me.

This book would not have been possible without the guidance and support of Melanie Falick. Thank you for encouraging my vision, which had been in my mind for a number of years. Working with you was both a pleasure and an honor. Sally Harding's keen edits and spot-on advice with the technical aspects of my designs were a most welcome addition. Jenny Hallengren's exquisite photography made my work come to life. Thank you for the care, time, and effort that you put into both photo shoots. Thank you to Sarah Gifford for her sensitive and beautiful design. Thank you also to Judith Huacuja for allowing and encouraging us to photograph part of the book at the University of Dayton. It was the perfect setting.

Thank you to my husband, Jeff, and our two amazing children, Aidan and Olivia. Jeff, you have always supported me and encouraged me to try new things, without ever batting an eye, and for that I am eternally grateful. You were my rock during the writing of this book, and I certainly couldn't have done it without you. Aidan and Olivia, you inspire me every day by how you see the world. I am lucky to be your mom, and you are my most incredible creations. Please know that there is nothing in this world that you cannot do if you work hard and put your mind to it. You three have my love forever.

RESOURCES

FABRIC

CLOTHWORKS AMERICAN MADE BRAND

http://americanmadebrand.com

FREESPIRIT

http://freespiritfabric.com

ROBERT KAUFMAN

http://www.robertkaufman.com

THREAD AND BATTING

AURIFIL

http://www.aurifil.com

COATS

http://www.makeitcoats.com

PELLON

http://www.pellonprojects.com

SKETCHBOOKS AND ART SUPPLIES

DICK BLICK

http://www.dickblick.com

PITT PEN MARKERS

http://www.fabercastell.com/art-and-graphic/artist-products/pitt-artist-pens

RHODIA SKETCHBOOKS

http://rhodiapads.com

ONLINE QUILTING AND SEWING CLASSES

CREATIVEBUG

http://www.creativebug.com

INSPIRATION

AMY BUTLER DESIGN

http://www.amybutlerdesign.com/

DENYSE SCHMIDT

http://dsquilts.com

FOLK FIBERS

http://www.folkfibers.com

THE MODERN QUILT GUILD

http://www.themodernquiltguild.com

QUILT ALLIANCE

http://www.allianceforamericanquilts.org

SHERRI LYNN WOOD

http://daintytime.net/

ONLINE FABRIC RETAILERS

CRIMSON TATE

https://www.crimsontate.com

FABRIC DEPOT

http://www.fabricdepot.com

THE FABRIC SHACK

http://www.fabricshack.com

HEATHER JONES has a master's degree (ABT) in art history from the University of Cincinnati. She is a quilt designer, teacher, and founder and former president of the Cincinnati Modern Quilt Guild. Her quilts have appeared in numerous publications, including *Martha Stewart Living* and *Modern Patchwork*. She teaches online at Creativebug.com, on television at Quilting Arts TV, and in person throughout the country.

Published in 2015 by Stewart, Tabori & Chang
An imprint of ABRAMS

Text © 2015 Heather Jones
Photographs © 2015 Jenny Hallengren

Library of Congress Control Number: 2014959124

ISBN: 978-1-61769-176-8

Editor: Melanie Falick
Designer: Sarah Gifford
Production Manager: True Sims

The text of this book was composed in LUX SANS, NATIONAL, and TYPEWRITER.

Printed and bound in China.
10 9 8 7 6 5 4 3 2 1

Stewart, Tabori & Chang books are available at special discounts when purchased in quantity for premiums and promotions as well as fundraising or educational use. Special editions can also be created to specification. For details, contact specialsales@abramsbooks.com or the address below.

THE ART OF BOOKS SINCE 1949
115 West 18th Street
New York, NY 10011
www.abramsbooks.com